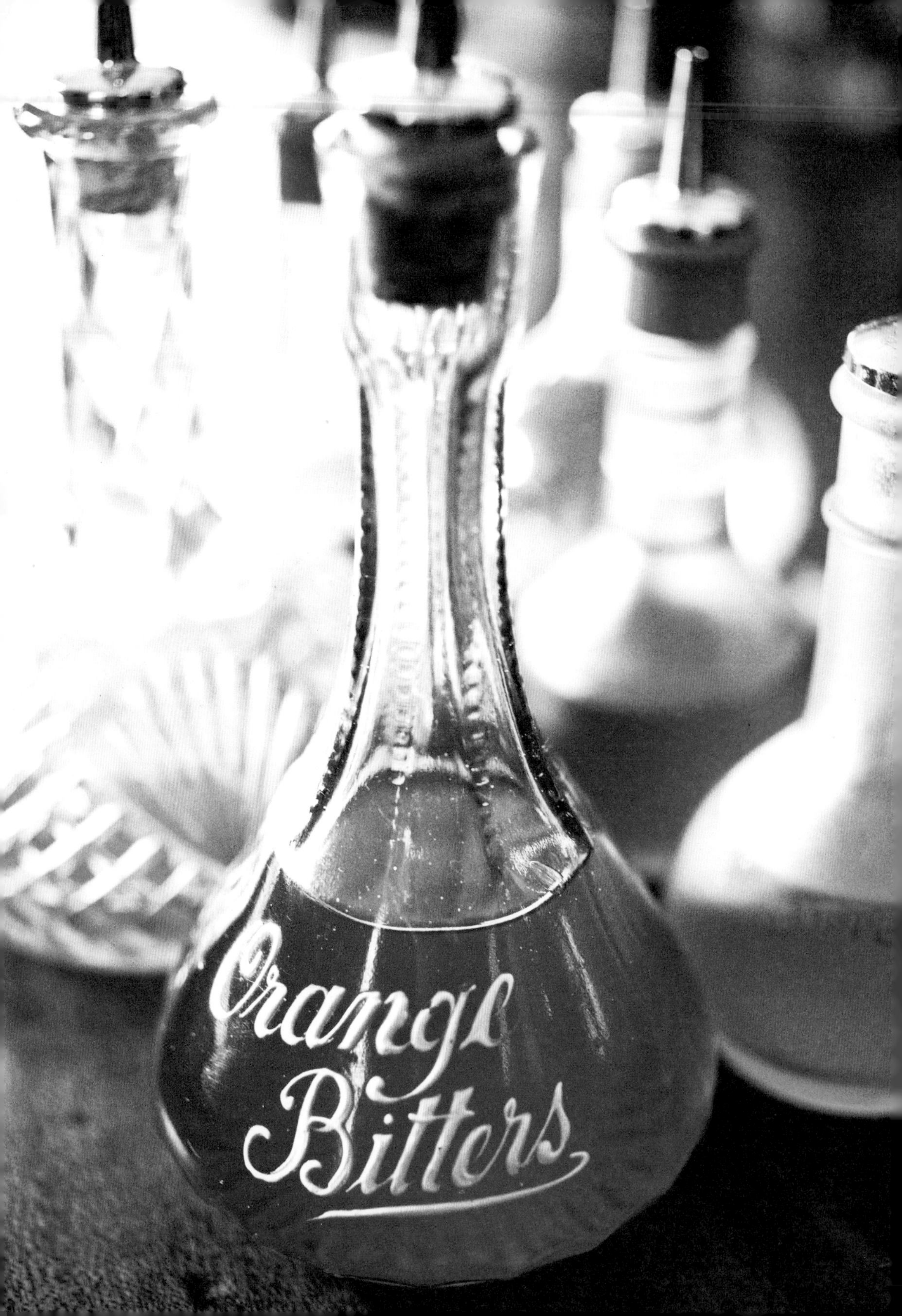
Orange
Bitters

A SPIRITED HISTORY
of a CLASSIC CURE~ALL

WITH

COCKTAILS, RECIPES
& FORMULAS

BITTERS

BRAD THOMAS PARSONS

PHOTOGRAPHS BY ED ANDERSON

TEN SPEED PRESS

BERKELEY

"*If you took the SAT exams back in the twentieth century, you may recall the curious puzzle 'Salt is to food, as bitters are to [blank].' What scholar had the bright idea that high school juniors knew how to mix a proper old-fashioned anyway?*"

KURT B. REIGHLEY, *UNITED STATES OF AMERICANA*

"*So drunk in the August sun, and you're the kind of girl I like...*"

PAVEMENT, "GOLD SOUNDZ"

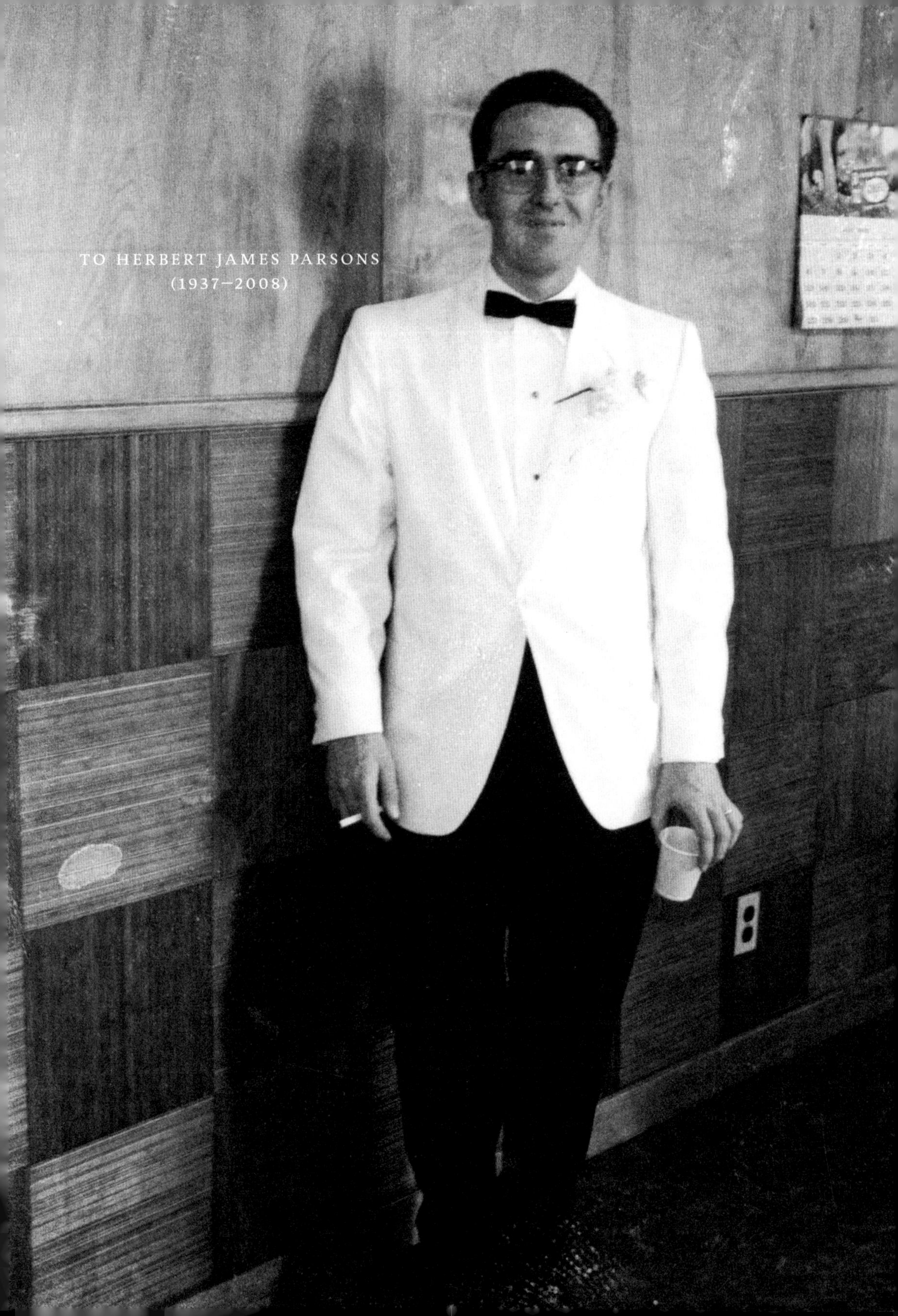

TO HERBERT JAMES PARSONS
(1937–2008)

A TABLE OF CONTENTS

INTRODUCTION

Cocktail culture has come a long way since I last worked behind the bar, which was in the early 1990s at Harpoon Eddie's in Sylvan Beach, New York, a town optimistically billed as "the Coney Island of Central New York." During college summer vacations I spent most of my shifts whipping up rum runners and strawberry daiquiris (by pressing a button on a constantly whirring machine that was eerily similar to the Slurpee station at a 7-Eleven), pulling endless pitchers of beer, and mixing innumerable Cape Codders. Our sour mix came out of a sticky soda gun, there was no such thing as simple syrup, and citrus juices were delivered to us in oversized cans from Sysco. I do remember a rarely reached-for bottle of Angostura bitters, with its distinctive yellow cap and oversized label, which was tucked away behind the house copy of *Mr. Boston: Official Bartender's Guide*. The only time I reached for the bitters was when Maurie, one of our regulars, ordered the occasional Manhattan, which I served in one of the four cocktail glasses we kept hanging on the rack (most of the beach-bound drinks were served in plastic cups). Granted, slinging drinks during your college years at a popular beach bar has its allure: 25-cent hot wing Wednesdays, beach volleyball tournaments, a prime seat for Fourth of July fireworks, plenty of bikinis, and decent tips. I try to make it back to Harpoon Eddie's at least once a summer when I'm back home, and I have a sneaking suspicion that the same bottle of bitters might still be behind the bar.

Most college students will drink whatever they can get their hands on—often to disastrous results (think grain alcohol holiday punch served from a Hefty bag–lined trash bin, spiked with peppermint schnapps and stained red from the box of candy canes the host dumped in as a garnish). In those days, my experience with what is now considered "speakeasy chic" was limited to the evenings when I would swing by the bar at the local members-only American Legion to ask my dad a favor (usually to borrow the car or twenty dollars; sometimes both). There the bartender would peer through the mirrored glass window to see who was at the door and buzz you in.

After several semesters of these ill-advised punches, fake IDs, and an excess of drinks that will never touch my lips again (I'm talking to you, Kahlúa and cream—and to any other cream-based drink that was pressed into my hands), it took me a long time to come to appreciate and understand the balance required of a proper cocktail. After college I cut my teeth on vodka martinis and vodka gimlets, but eventually I embraced brown spirits, especially bourbon and rye, and then, as a fully formed adult, I moved onto the pleasures of aperitifs and digestifs flavored with bitters, herbs, and botanicals.

* * * *

Aromatic cocktail bitters—the kind you don't sip but add in dashes to enliven a drink—were an essential ingredient in classic cocktails, and are now back and bigger than ever. Just as restaurant menus herald the local farmer who grew the heirloom carrots featured in that night's special, cocktail menus increasingly single out house-made bitters and those made by artisanal producers. And indeed, seeking out the best bitters can become as much of an obsession as finding the freshest locally sourced ingredients. The same DIY ethos that made growing tomatoes on your apartment's rooftop, making your own seasonal preserves, curing charcuterie on your fire escape, and all sorts of other hands-on kitchen projects so popular over the past five or so years has rolled out to bars. Today listing house-made bitters on the menu and displaying dozens of homemade tinctures is a benchmark for most serious bar programs. Once I've sized up a joint, I'll ask the bartender, "Do you make your own bitters?" More often than not the answer is yes: orange, grapefruit, coffee, barley, cherry-vanilla, plum, rhubarb, rosemary, and lavender, to name just a few.

Asking that simple question makes me feel connected to an ongoing conversation about the history of the American cocktail. And it's not just because the bartender is decked out in his nineteenth-century best and most likely sporting a Civil War–era beard or artfully waxed mustache. It's because that simple old-fashioned—the one made with rye, simple syrup, bitters, and a lemon twist—is practically what you would be holding in your hand if you walked into a bar in the late 1800s and Jerry Thomas served you himself.

* * * *

In 2009 I wrote a short piece on homemade bitters for *Seattle Met* magazine. I quickly geeked out on the topic, and sharing my enthusiasm with so many bartenders who were also on the bitters trail only increased my obsession. At the bar Spur in Seattle, where David Nelson was bartending

when I wrote the piece (bartenders, like ballplayers, move around to other teams all the time), there were nearly two dozen squat glass bottles lining the bar, each filled with one of Nelson's homemade bitters and tinctures. When David said, "You know, it would be pretty ingenious if someone wrote a book on bitters," his words stuck with me, and I shared David's sentiment with my friend A. J. Rathbun, who writes a new cocktail book nearly every year. He smiled and said, "Don't look at me. That's all you, my friend." That night I revisited my dog-eared copy of *Imbibe!*, David Wondrich's award-winning historical biography of Jerry Thomas, America's first celebrity bartender and the man who in 1862 published the first known collection of cocktail recipes. I came across this quote in Wondrich's book: "As for the bitters and syrups, were these to receive the attention they deserve, they would easily fill another volume the size of this one." That sealed the deal for me. I was a man on a mission. It was fortunate that I got into the bitters game just as they were reclaiming their proper place behind the bar.

When I'm into something—a band, a book, a bourbon—I tend to get a bit obsessed. Growing up (and even well into adulthood), I collected *Star Wars* action figures. And that same completist spirit—needing to have every variation of every character—came back to me as I tracked down as many bitters as I could, both in stores and online. As soon as a new brand or flavor came on the market, I would scoop it up and take it home to experiment. I researched and tracked down old bitters recipes online and in vintage cocktail books to make my own bitters at home, and I scored samples of new releases and homemade bitters from bartending friends. Today I consider my bitters collection pretty impressive, but there's still more out there, and more coming on the market every month. And there are still those holy grail bitters to track down, bitters that keep my quest alive: securing an unopened bottle of Suntory Hermes Orange Bitters from Japan is almost as impossible as finding the elusive 1979 mail-order rocket-firing Boba Fett.

* * * *

One evening at the Seattle bar Vessel, as bartenders Jim Romdall and Keith Waldbauer were passing me sample-size bottles of new bitters to try, Keith said to me, "You know, by the time your bitters book comes out, it's already going to be out of date." A lesser man might have been discouraged by Keith's remark, or the idea that a book won't be able to keep up with all the new bitters entering the marketplace, but I actually think his words point to something exciting. As recently as 2003, there were only a handful of bitters available commercially, and it had been that way for more than 150 years, but now there are dozens of new flavors just a mouse click away. To stay abreast of new bitters trends, visit my website www.btparsons.com, where I'll keep you up to date on any new bitters that enter the marketplace.

After reading news about this book, a cocktail writer posted on Twitter, "A whole book on bitters? I'm incredulous and delighted." If this book inspires you to dig out that bottle of Angostura from the back of your cupboard or seek out an orange or celery or grapefruit bitters to play around with at home, then I've done my job, and I will be equally delighted.

1

A BRIEF
HISTORY OF
BITTERS

If you've stepped into a neo-speakeasy or perused the menu at a cocktail lounge specializing in classic drinks in the last few years, you might have noticed that the cocktail world is in the midst of a bitters boom. Dozens of artisanal and craft bitters makers have introduced new small-batch bitters to the market, and hundreds of individual bartenders and cocktail enthusiasts are experimenting with making their own homemade bitters. Today, instead of that lone bottle of Angostura bitters holding court behind the bar, myriad bitters are lined up on the bar in decorative glass bottles waiting to be put to creative use. Although just ten years ago locating a bottle of orange bitters would have been as likely as stumbling upon the Fountain of Youth, you can now choose from many different brands of orange bitters to recreate a classic Bijou (page 120) or Alaska Cocktail (page 117) or to bring a dash of complexity to a classic martini (page 132). Considering that as recently as 2004 there were only three commercial brands of bitters still standing, this is fantastic news for devoted drinkers.

The dearth of bitters throughout much of the twentieth century is quite shocking, especially when you consider that hundreds of different brands were in use up through Prohibition. Historically, bitters were considered an essential element to a cocktail: they even play a part in the first written definition of the word "cocktail," which can be found in the May 13, 1806, edition of the Federalist newspaper *The Balance, and Columbian Repository* of Hudson, New York. The editor, responding to a reader's letter about a previous article using the word "cock-tail" to describe one of the drinks served to lubricate voters at a political rally, wrote, "Cocktail is a stimulating liquor composed of spirits of any kind, sugar, water, and bitters—it is vulgarly called a bittered sling and is supposed to be an excellent electioneering potion, inasmuch as it renders the heart stout and bold, at the same time that it fuddles the head."

"Cocktail," then, was just another classification for a specific type of drink in a lexicon that already included such colorful categories as the julep, smash, toddy, fizz, daisy, cobbler, sling, sour, and flip, among others. Since 1806 the word "cocktail" has evolved into a catchall for nearly any mixed drink containing spirits, from a martini to an appletini and everything in between.

But even before it had a name, people were already drinking that combination of spirits, alcohol, water, and sugar. And before being listed as an ingredient in the so-called "cock-tail," bitters were consumed on their own, drunk not in a dash but in a gulp or in a glass as a patent medicine.

Sometime in the late eighteenth century, however, drinkers began to add the already high-proof bitters to alcohol rather than consuming them on their own. Although the cocktail and what would become known as cocktail bitters gained popularity in colonial America, drinks historian David Wondrich, author of *Imbibe!* and *Punch*, doesn't believe that the cocktail was an American invention. Pointing out the popularity of England's Stoughton Bitters, which was patented in 1712, Wondrich suggests, "I think the cocktail goes back to London in the early 1700s, when patent bitters were first being advertised as a hangover cure when mixed with Canary wine or brandy. By 1750, they were being mixed with burnt brandy, which was made by lighting brandy on fire and melting sugar into it. So functionally— mixologically, if you will—there was already a cocktail in England by 1750." Although this might be the case, it is also true that colonial America embraced the cocktail and helped bitters make the leap from patent medicine to flavoring agent.

DEMYSTIFYING BITTERS

So what, exactly, are bitters? Bitters are an aromatic flavoring agent made from infusing roots, barks, fruit peels, seeds, spices, herbs, flowers, and botanicals in high-proof alcohol (or sometimes glycerin). Long reputed to possess medicinal properties, bitters were billed as the cure for whatever ailed you, whether it was a headache, indigestion, stomach cramps, or constipation. Using bitter herbs, barks, and botanicals for medicinal purposes dates back centuries, and versions of some of these potable elixirs are still around today, like the herbal liqueur Chartreuse, which was first made in 1737 by Carthusian monks who based their recipe on an ancient elixir presented to them by François Hannibal d'Estrées in 1605. (Indeed, it took the monks over a century to "unravel the complexities" of the ancient recipe.)

The tongue's taste buds allow humans to discern five distinct flavors: sweet, salty, sour, bitter, and savory (or umami). Humans and many animals are hardwired to be averse to bitter flavors, since they're a warning signal that what you're about to ingest might be toxic. But bitterness can also be alluring, especially when it's delivered through coffee, chocolate, eggplant, grapefruit, hops, artichokes, and naturally bitter herbs and lettuces. In *The*

Flavor Bible, Karen Page and Andrew Dornenburg point out that many chefs view bitterness as "an indispensable 'cleansing' taste—one that makes you want to take the next bite, and the next."

One of the biggest misconceptions about bitters is that using them will make your drink bitter. Although this is understandable—tasted by themselves, bitters often taste slightly bitter or bittersweet—the term "bitters" refers not to a specific flavor but rather to the category of aromatic solutions made with bittering agents such as gentian root and cinchona bark. Bitters are essentially a liquid seasoning agent for drinks and even food, and their frequent description as a bartender's salt and pepper hits close to the mark. Make two Manhattans—one with rye, sweet vermouth, and Angostura bitters, and one without the bitters—and taste them side by side. You'll notice the difference. A Manhattan isn't palatable without bitters; it's just an overly sweet drink lacking the depth and spicy nuance brought on by a dash or two of bitters. Bitters are the ultimate matchmaker: just a dash or two can bring a perfect balance to two seemingly incompatible spirits. Adding bitters can tamp down an overly sweet drink, help cut through richness, unite disparate ingredients, and add an aromatic spiciness.

Seattle bartender and bitters aficionado Jamie Boudreau maintains, "If I ever feel that a cocktail is flat or missing something, the answer is almost always bitters. Just a dash will usually help balance a slightly sweet drink and also offer a complexity that may have been missing before." A. J. Rathbun, who has authored a number of cocktail books, including *Good Spirits* and *Luscious Liqueurs*, offers his spin on what bitters do for a drink: "I like to think that different bitters might serve different functions, depending on herbal notes and character and personality and how well they stand out in the mix versus using their powers to alter other flavors. Overall, I think that bitters really do help other ingredients work together and to get acquainted in a way that leads to a long-lasting friendship, one that equals more as a whole than as individual parts."

Aromatic bitters, when applied to a cocktail in a measure of dashes as a unifying ingredient, are known as "cocktail bitters." This is in contrast to potable bitters that are intended to be sipped on their own as an aperitif to stimulate the appetite or as a digestif to help aid digestion. This book focuses on aromatic cocktail bitters. Unlike potable bitters like Campari, Fernet Branca, Jägermeister, and Averna, which are meant to sipped on their own or mixed into a drink in a measure of ounces rather than dashes, nonpotable bitters are too high in alcohol and too concentrated in flavor to be taken in

Bitters and Soda

My friend Amy isn't the only person I know who swears by the restorative powers of bitters and soda, but she puts this belief into action more than anyone else I know. When we're at a party or having dinner out, even if she's drinking a cocktail or a glass of wine, she always keeps a bitters and soda within arm's reach.

And she's on to something. Bitters and soda is the requisite drink when you've had a gut-busting evening of overindulgence. I experienced such a night at a Seattle party for New Orleans chef John Besh. He was in town cooking for a small group, presenting dishes from his cookbook, *My New Orleans*. It was an honor to be sampling his culinary creations so far from the Big Easy, cooked by the man himself, but after crab-stuffed artichokes, seconds of barbecued shrimp, and crawfish agnolotti, I had to cry uncle midway through the roasted baby goat with spring vegetables over grits (though I did manage to make room for the strawberry shortcake).

As soon as I walked through the door of my apartment, I went to the bar and, in a nod to New Orleans, pulled out the Peychaud's Bitters. Two tall glasses of bitters and soda was just what I needed to spring me from my food coma.

Fill a tall glass with ice. Armed with your bitters of choice, let loose with four to six vigorous shakes over the ice and then top with club soda or seltzer. Repeat as needed.

Makes 1 drink

4 to 6 dashes bitters

Club soda or seltzer

more than a dash (although some bartenders are known to knock back a full shot glass of Angostura bitters at the end of their shift to prove their mettle).

FURTHER RESTORATIVE CLAIMS

Bartenders swear that Angostura is a no-fail cure for the hiccups. Simply soak a sugar-coated lemon wedge with Angostura and ask the afflicted to take a bite. Admittedly, this remedy is only good when you have all of the ingredients handy, so hopefully your next case of the hiccups hits you when you're chatting up your local bartender.

A BOUNTY OF BITTERS

As David Wondrich has pointed out, bitters were being applied to spirituous drinks in England in the late 1700s, but the bitters boom really exploded in the United States in the 1850s. The dasher top wasn't in use yet. Instead, bitters were still being nipped from the bottle or added to a drink with a pour rather than doled out in dashes and drops. Bitters were still considered medicinal, so it was like taking a slug of NyQuil; plus the flavorful bitters helped wash down inferior booze. The increased taxes on the sale of alcohol coupled with the rise of the early temperance movement actually helped bitters' popularity. The tax laws and the temperance movement made drinking socially unacceptable in many circles, but it was considered normal behavior to have a daily nip of stomach bitters, whose real kick and purported medical benefits were lubricated by high-proof alcohol. Historically, alcohol-based bitters were classified as nonpotable alcohol and weren't affected by taxes aimed at the sales of spirits, and the same is true today.

By the mid-nineteenth century there were hundreds of bitters available, most still making outrageous claims to cure any ailment from indigestion to malaria. As advertising for these snake oils flourished, the curative promises become more exaggerated (including, for example, one vintage advertisement's promise to "strengthen, invigorate, tone, and rebuild the entire system"). Bitters became a multimillion-dollar industry, and knockoff versions of popular brands began to pop up. Wondrich points out that having your bitters coupled with alcohol tasted good, "plus it allowed you to claim that you were taking your morning drink strictly for medical reasons"—a phenomenon that should be familiar to anyone living in the overprescribed, pill-popping nation that is modern America.

Dr. J. Hostetter's Stomach Bitters, which began production out of Lancaster, Pennsylvania, in 1853, was one of the most popular bitters of its time, and at 47 percent alcohol, it isn't hard to believe that even though it was classified as medicinal, it was being sold by the shot in Alaska saloons. During the Civil War, Union troops were receiving it by the train-carload and using it not only as "a positive protective against the fatal maladies of the Southern swamps, and the poisonous tendency of the impure rivers and bayous," but also for liquid courage on the battlefield. Hostetter's is believed to have been selling more than six thousand bottles of bitters a day after 1865.

Abbott's Bitters, based out of Baltimore, Maryland, is rumored to be the bitters used in the original Manhattan recipe, and for a time it was positioned to be one of the bitters that would have a long shelf life. It lasted until the early 1950s, and serves as a case for why branding bitters became so important. Bitters were a lucrative business, and knockoff brands weren't uncommon. In the case of Siegert v. Abbott, the two bitters manufacturers fought over the use of the word "Angostura" in their name (it refers to both an ingredient in the bitters and to the town in Venezuela where they were made). After losing the case, Abbott's had to change their labels and advertising, while Siegert's Angostura went on to become the go-to bitters, the Angostura aromatic bitters that's still around today. Despite the trademark lawsuit, Abbott's actually survived Prohibition, but due to poor business management the brand dried up in the 1940s, and now it lives on only in memory, and on online auction sites.

Other bitters of the pre-Prohibition era include Boker's Bitters, Boonekamp's Bitters, Koosh Bitters, and Baxter's Mandrake Bitters. Bitters like Atwood's Jaundice Bitters and Porter's Stomach Bitters were aimed at specific organs and ailments, such as the kidney, liver, and blood. Although most of them probably used a similar base of herbs and botanicals, there was so much room to play around with the flavor profile that it's impossible to know what each of these tasted like. I imagine they were pretty

Tasting Abbott's

I got my first taste of Abbott's Bitters thanks to Jim Meehan, the lauded mixologist who runs PDT (Please Don't Tell) in Manhattan's East Village. When you walk down St. Marks Place you'll see the hot-dog-shaped sign for Crif Dogs, with "Eat Me" spelled out in mustard yellow. Walk down the steps, past the vintage arcade games, and you'll notice a phone booth on your left. Savvy drinkers know that when you push open the door to that booth, pick up the orange phone, and give the dial a spin, the door on the other side of the booth will open to reveal a hostess. If there's room in the bar, she'll invite you inside. If not, she'll add your phone number to her wait list. PDT does take same-day reservations starting promptly at 3 P.M. but, fair warning, you might be hitting redial for a while to get through. Once you're inside, you'll be enveloped in a warm, clubby atmosphere with the soft buzz of happy customers drinking delicious cocktails.

I came by in the afternoon and for hours we sat across from each other as Jim laid out dozens of bitters to sample (every guy who makes his own bitters sends them to Jim in the hopes of landing them on the PDT menu). Jim pulled out limited-edition, industry-only bitters made by Germany's The Bitter Truth, multiple bottles of Peruvian bitters, and early samples from Bittermens as he pointed out some of the subtle differences among early samples of their Xocolatl Mole Bitters, later samples, and the cobranded version created and distributed by The Bitter Truth.

But the ultimate taste test came when Jim produced an antique bottle of Abbott's Bitters that he had won in an eBay auction. The bottle, which was of 1920s vintage, had been filled with bitters (minus what had evaporated over ninety years) when he bought it. Now, though, the bottle was nearly empty. Jim explained that it had accidentally fallen off his desk, spilling most of its precious liquid on the floor.

wince-inducing, though, if only because of their claims to cure anything and everything, including fever sores, constipation, palpitations, jaundice, colds, coughs, dullness, and flatulence.

An ad for Mishler's Herb Bitters ("The Great Household Remedy") is pretty representative of bitters' cure-all claims: "Mishler's Herb Bitters is

"I'm going to give this to you," Jim said, cupping the bottle between his hands. "I want you to have it. It's good karma. Once you try Abbott's you'll shed a tear about something amazing being gone."

Three hours later, as I was gathering my things, Jim cracked open the bottle, which barely had two dashes left, and handed it to me. "I want you to try a little dash of this and then let me make you a Manhattan and send you on your merry way. Put a little bit on your finger." I did. The barrel-aged aroma was intense and spicy, with clove, cinnamon, and anise popping through on the tongue. "Isn't that insane?"

He then went to work on making two Manhattans, setting a bottle of Dolin sweet vermouth on the bar and reaching to the top shelf for a bottle of 15-year Pappy Van Winkle bourbon ("this is Chang's bottle"). "It's 'fiddy-fiddy,'" he explained, pouring the Manhattans into two chilled coupe glasses, "instead of 2:1, which is what I would normally do. It's not your classic Carpano Antica and rye." We clinked our glasses and took a sip. A second of silence and then a wry smile from Jim, "Well, it doesn't suck."

endorsed by physicians, sold by druggists, and possesses the confidence of the people. In all cases of Dyspepsia, Liver Complaint, Kidney Disease, Loss of Nervous Energy, Sexual Weakness, Diarrhea, etc., it will be found a reliable remedy. It is certain and uniform in its effects. It has cured thousands and it will cure YOU. Try it." That's one mighty potent "etc." in there.

PEYCHAUD'S BITTERS

When discussing a bitters landscape that fairly quickly went from hundreds of brands to just a handful of survivors, one must mention Mr. Antoine Amedie Peychaud, a Creole immigrant from San Domingo (now Haiti) who played a vital role in the history of bitters and of an iconic American cocktail. As a pharmacist, Peychaud was versed in the curative powers of herbs and botanicals. He soon perfected a proprietary bitters based on a family recipe, which in 1838 he began dispensing at his apothecary at 437 Royal Street in New Orleans's French Quarter. He became well known for administering Cognac spiced with his house bitters in a double-ended egg cup, or jigger, called a *coquetier*. Stanley Clisby Arthur, in *Famous New Orleans Drinks and How to Mix 'Em*, offers that "possibly through sampling too many of M. Peychaud's spiced brandies, the thickened tongues of the imbibers slurred the word [*coquetier*] into 'cocktail.'"

Soon people began requesting Peychaud's Bitters by name in the city's popular coffeehouses (the 1800s term for establishments in the business of selling alcoholic drinks). New Orleans's most famous cocktail was born at the Sazerac Coffee House on Exchange Alley, where, in 1850, owner Sewell Taylor applied Peychaud's exclusively to Sazerac de Forge et Fils Cognac, which he imported from France and sold exclusively, and soon the drink became synonymous with the name of the establishment.

In 1869 Thomas H. Handy purchased the Sazerac Coffee House, and then in 1873 he bought the exclusive rights to Peychaud's Bitters. To this day the Sazerac Company still distributes these historic bitters, which, along with Angostura, was one of the only brands of bitters to survive Prohibition. It's said that part of the reason Peychaud's never fell out of favor is thanks to New Orleans's private drinking clubs, where it was, and remains, an essential ingredient for a Sazerac (page 112) and another New Orleans favorite, the Vieux Carré (page 148), in addition to the Seelbach Cocktail (page 146). While classified as an aromatic bitters, Peychaud's isn't as deeply seasoned as Angostura but is more floral, with a light cherry spice and a heady anise flavor. Its bright red cough-syrup color also helps it stand out from the competition, and just a few dashes can cause a cocktail to take on its trademark candy-apple blush.

ANGOSTURA AROMATIC BITTERS

Some say that Peychaud's was the first commercial bitters, but in terms of popularity and global ubiquity, the prize goes to the famously yellow-capped Angostura aromatic bitters. The man behind the best-known bitters around the world was Johann Gottlieb Benjamin Siegert, a German doctor who studied medicine at the University of Berlin and served under Marshal von Blücher at the Battle of Waterloo. In 1820 the adventurous doctor left for Venezuela, where he was appointed surgeon general in Simón Bolívar's army, based out of the town of Angostura (now Ciudad Bolívar). Using his medical knowledge, Siegert harvested many of the local herbs, roots, botanicals, and barks (but not, despite the name, the bark of the angostura tree) to create tonics to stimulate the appetite of the troops, aid with digestive distress, and keep the army on its feet. By 1824 he had perfected a proprietary blend of Siegert's Amargo Aromatico (aromatic bitters).

Because it was a trading post on the Orinoco River, the town of Angostura (meaning "the narrows") saw a brisk maritime activity as ships set sail for locations throughout the Caribbean. Soon Siegert's bitters were being used by sailors to quell seasickness, and word of his product spread. By 1830 his bitters were available not only in nearby Trinidad but as far away as England. By 1850 the good doctor had retired from military service to focus full-time on his bitters business. After his sons Alfredo and Carlos entered the family business they changed its name to Dr. J.G.B. Siegert & Hijos. Don Carlos, as Carlos Siegert became known, described in official Angostura historical notes as a "bon vivant, impeccable in his dress and manners," helped expand the brand by presenting the bitters at world expositions. Dr. Siegert died in 1870 and, due to increasing political strife and instability, the family moved the business from Venezuela to nearby Trinidad, whereupon brother Luis joined, and where the company is located to this day. Carlos died in 1903 and Luis in 1905, leaving Alfredo in charge.

After he took his business public, Alfredo proved to lack the business acumen of his brothers and father, and the company wound up in the hands of creditors. But the House of Angostura persevered, and its bitters, with their distinctive oversized label, remain today an integral ingredient in many classic cocktails, such as the old-fashioned, the Manhattan, and the Champagne Cocktail. The original formula remains a company secret, known to only five people.

ABOUT THAT ANGOSTURA LABEL

The oversized paper label pasted on a bottle of Angostura aromatic bitters could be considered a trademark in its own right. There are several stories about its origin, but the two most popular suggest that it's the result of the laid-back Caribbean attitude of the House of Angostura. In one version, the wrong label was applied to the bottle and the problem was never corrected. In the other, the person responsible for ordering the bottles never communicated with the person responsible for ordering the labels. Either way, the label remains today as it was a hundred years ago.

A BITTER LANDSCAPE

After years of so many far-fetched claims of healing and restorative powers, it was inevitable that bitters makers were going to be called out. Congress passed the Pure Food and Drug Act of 1906, which was enacted to prevent "the manufacture, sale, or transportation of adulterated or misbranded or poisonous or deleterious foods, drugs, medicines, and liquors, and for regulating traffic therein, and for other purposes." Bitters, which mostly had been sold as unregulated patent medicines, now had to clearly label their ingredients. Words like "cure" were removed from labels, lower alcohol limits were put into place, and the bitters business took a blow from which it never really recovered. This immediately affected the snake-oil-style patent medicine bitters, which were effectively shunned from the marketplace, and thus opened up the playing field for more reputable brands such as Abbott's, Boker's, and Angostura, which had been adopted behind the bar.

With the passing of the Volstead Act in 1919 and the arrival of Prohibition, though, bitters' knockout was complete. Aside from Peychaud's, Angostura, and a handful of orange bitters, the product all but evaporated. The Pure Food and Drug Act had stripped away the morning medicine nips of bitters, and even the bitters being used behind the bar were now associated with illegal activity. More importantly, the cocktail scene changed. Some speakeasies were certainly glamorous, with secret words and flappers dancing to a riveting jazz score, but most were simply dark basements where you stood the chance of getting seriously ill from the illicit booze you imbibed. Prohibition may not have stopped people from drinking, but it did change *what* they were drinking. Bartenders no longer felt the need to add a subtle dash of bitters to elevate and enliven a cocktail; instead, they added potent juices and syrups to mask the taste of low-quality alcohol. Bartenders stopped adding bitters to many drinks in which they had been used before, and new drinks being created simply didn't call for them at all. Organized crime rings controlled the black market for liquor, and distilleries dried up. Bartending, once considered a skilled craft, became an illegal, underground activity, and the sense of pride and showmanship went along with the bartenders who took their trade to Europe and Cuba.

The Noble Experiment proved to be anything but, and when the Eighteenth Amendment was finally repealed, cocktail culture and the bitters scene had been dealt a defeat that would take decades to begin to recover from.

The Great Angostura Shortage
of 2009–2010

In January 2010, the *New York Post* sounded the alarm: "Manhattan Cocktail Faces Bitter End." Would it really be impossible to order a Manhattan in Manhattan (or Brooklyn, for that matter)?

The period of about six months from fall 2009 through spring 2010—dubbed "Bittersgate" and the "Angosturapocalypse" by some—was an uneasy time for bartenders and bitters lovers as the world experienced a shortage of Angostura bitters. There were rumors of a strike at the House of Angostura in Trinidad; of financial restructuring of the parent company, the CL Financial Group; of emergency government bailouts in Trinidad and Tobago; and of problems sourcing the herbs, spices, and botanicals that go into the top-secret Angostura formula. Angostura assured distributors that more cases would be coming, but the shelves remained empty.

During the shortage I would stop by DeLaurenti, an Italian gourmet store in Seattle's Pike Place Market, every Saturday to see how things were faring. They carried the best selection of bitters in the city, but, like victims in an Agatha Christie novel, the Angostura bottles were dropping off the shelf one by one. Finally there was just an empty shelf. The same thing was happening in grocery stores all over the city.

And where there are empty shelves there is hoarding and online price gouging. While I didn't go into full stockpiling mode, I did tuck away a few extra bottles (I was writing this book, after all). Bartenders knew to stock up before the supply dried up. Restaurant supply stores proved to be an off-the-radar source, but soon they dried up as well.

While a bottle of Angostura might last for years in a home liquor cabinet, a busy bar specializing in the classics can run through a bottle in a week, or even a few days. And this was happening at the height of the American cocktail revival, when so many vintage drinks were calling for that pivotal dash of bitters to make the drink shine. The old-fashioned and Manhattan couldn't exist without bitters, and the same goes for the Champagne Cocktail, which is made with a bitters-soaked sugar cube.

This unexpected shortage of Angostura proved to be an opportunity for smaller makers of bitters, such as Fee Brothers in Rochester, New York, and Germany's The Bitter Truth, to grab the mic and build customer awareness with a shout of, "Hey, look, Angostura isn't the only bitters in town." But even if The Bitter Truth's Jerry Thomas' Own Decanter Bitters could come off the bench and be a designated bitters for your Manhattan, or a few dashes of Fee Brothers Old Fashion Aromatic Bitters could revive an Angostura-less old-fashioned, the shortage reminded cocktail enthusiasts everywhere that there is no replacement for Angostura. As Coca-Cola is to cola, Angostura is to bitters.

Viewers of MSNBC's *The Rachel Maddow Show* have likely noticed that the affable host is a serious student of the American cocktail and sometimes wraps up an hour of pop-culture-infused political commentary with a segment called the Cocktail Moment, where she'll geek out about the history of cocktails, celebrate a particular spirit, or welcome a guest bartender for an in-studio demonstration.

She required Angostura bitters for a St. Patrick's Day cocktail demonstration and quickly realized that the city was dry. She marveled, "Why are there no bitters in all of Manhattan?" Soon after that segment Maddow was presented with a care package from Angostura, and she posted a photo of herself online with an expression of pure joy as she held up to the camera six bottles of Angostura.

Then, on April 15, 2010, she welcomed two very special guests for the Cocktail Moment segment. After expertly mixing a Manhattan and assembling a Champagne Cocktail, she praised the power of the common denominator in those two drinks: Angostura bitters. She then introduced two executives from Angostura: Genevieve Jodhan, executive manager of export sales and business development, and Giselle Laronde-West, the communications manager. It was announced that the Great Angostura Shortage was over. The legendary liquid had never dried up, as rumored. The shortage was caused by the unfortunate combination of a supply issue with the company that manufactured the bottles coupled with a spike in demand for the product. Things had gotten back on track the previous January, when the company switched to a new bottle supplier in China, and by April Angostura was back on the shelves.

As Maddow said, "Sometimes it takes breaking up to realize how in love you were."

2

A BITTERS
BOOM

COCKTAIL GEEKS, VINTAGE BAR BOOKS, AND THE INTERNET

Following World War II and into the 1950s, Angostura and Peychaud's were the only two major bitters still standing until Fee Brothers, based in Rochester, New York, came out with a basic aromatic bitters and an orange bitters in 1951. Fee Brothers had stayed in business during Prohibition by positioning themselves in a number of legal alcohol-related businesses. Their syrups and flavorings were put to use by illegal establishments who were in need of making illegal—and often unpalatable—spirits more appealing to their underground customers. Fee Brothers also produced communion wine for churches and served as sales representatives and consultants to citizens, who could still legally produce limited batches of wine for private consumption in their homes. They also sold a nonalcoholic beer that came with the cheeky warning, "Do not add yeast to this product as it is likely to ferment."

While the repeal of Prohibition allowed people to produce, sell, and consume alcohol legally, the art of mixology had suffered, and some would say that even with today's cocktail renaissance, the damaging effects of Prohibition are still being felt. Byzantine liquor laws that differ from state to state are one major aftershock of Prohibition.

Although many original cocktails were invented out of necessity during Prohibition, certain spirits like rye, whose distilleries had been shut down, became less popular because they were less available. In the 1960s vodka instead of gin became the spirit of choice in a martini, and the use of bitters in cocktails was limited to a few classics such as the Manhattan and the old-fashioned. Joe Fee, the great-grandson of Fee Brothers' founder Joseph Fee, explains that the labels and bottles for their new line of bitters just sat there due to lack of demand. As the years went by, the bitters situation remained the same. "It was all about the piña colada during the disco era," Fee explains. "The blender took over our imagination behind the bar. Bitters in general just folded from view. Then along came the Internet and everything changed."

But it was back in the late 1980s, before e-mail and Google and online auction sites, when the debonair Dale DeGroff (now rightfully known as "King Cocktail") played a pivotal role in the rebirth of classic cocktails. In 1987 DeGroff was behind the bar at New York's storied Rainbow Room, where, working with legendary restaurateur Joe Baum, he helped develop a beverage program that eschewed the popular commercial mixers and syrups in favor of fresh ingredients. A tattered edition of Jerry Thomas's 1862 book, *The Bartender's Guide: How to Mix Drinks or The Bon Vivant's Companion*, served as DeGroff's primary reference for understanding the classics before reinterpreting them with his own modern touch. Thomas's book and other old bartending manuals also highlighted the craft and technique of bartending, skills that DeGroff developed and that led him to become an inspiration to younger bartenders, who look upon him as a modern-day Jerry Thomas.

DeGroff set the precedent, and soon others followed. In the early 1990s self-described "cocktail freaks" Gary and Mardee Regan, who have gone on to write extensively about spirits and authored several must-own books on mixology, couldn't find an orange bitters to use in classic cocktails, so they decided to make their own. Using a recipe from Charles H. Baker Jr.'s out-of-print 1939 book, *The Gentleman's Companion*, as a jumping-off point, Gary Regan began experimenting, running around New York to track down strange herbs and botanicals. The recipe appeared as Regans' Orange Bitters No. 4 in their 1998 book, *The Book of Bourbon*. But Gary soon discovered that the recipe wasn't ready for prime time: it was far too bitter. He went back to the "lab," but this time he enlisted the services of Mark Brown, the president and CEO of the Sazerac Company of New Orleans. A partnership was formed and a recipe that worked for everyone was developed, but the Tax and Trade Bureau thought it was too potable—it was so tasty that people might knock it back straight from the bottle rather than employ a concentrated dash to their drink. This particular recipe, Regans' Orange Bitters No. 5, was shared in Gary Regan's 2003 book, *The Joy of Mixology*, and has since been used as a starting point for a generation of modern mixologists looking to experiment with making their own bitters. In 2005 Regans' Orange Bitters No. 6 went on the market, the first new bitters commercially available since the Fee Brothers produced theirs fifty years earlier.

Cocktail geek Ted Haigh, known as "Dr. Cocktail," chronicled his own quest to track down orange bitters in the 1990s in his book *Vintage Spirits and Forgotten Cocktails: From the Alamagoozlum Cocktail to the Zombie*. This led him to John "Jack" Fee, the grandson of Joseph Fee. Orange bitters were still being produced by Fee Brothers, but people either didn't know or didn't care, so they weren't generally available. Ted points out in his book that

after he placed his phone order, the only way Fee Brothers was set up to take payment was by billing him thirty days net. In 2006 the orange bitters market further expanded with the arrival of The Bitter Truth Orange Bitters from German bartenders and bitters makers Stephan Berg and Alexander Hauck. This was followed in 2008 by the long-rumored release of Angostura orange bitters, Angostura's first new bitters in over 180 years.

The burgeoning interest in the cocktail culture of the past sent bartenders and serious cocktail enthusiasts to eBay, online discussion boards, and stores selling used and collectible books to seek out old recipes. And what they discovered was that many vital ingredients, especially bitters, were no longer available.

A DASH TO MARKET: TODAY'S BITTERS MAKERS

Angostura may be the original "must-have" bitters, but these days there are scores of unique commercial and small-batch bitters available to keep those yellow-capped bottles company on the shelf. You can find most of the following bitters online, in bar supply stores, or in specialty groceries, but the thrill of the hunt is part of what makes them so special.

Fee Brothers (Rochester, New York)

Fee Brothers has been around since 1863 (hence their motto, "The House of Fee by the Genesee since eighteen hundred and sixty-three") and deserve their reputation as "keepers of the flame," as Robert Hess puts it, for continuing to produce bitters long after most bitters makers dried up (their Old Fashion Aromatic Bitters and West Indian Orange Bitters have been in production since 1951). Joe Fee, who with his sister Ellen Fee represents the fourth generation of bitters-making Fees, tells me that the company's annual bitters output in those days was a mere five gallons a year. But with the cocktail revival and the consequent bitters boom, the Fees have been able to expand their line of flavored bitters. Popular products in the Fee Brothers line include their Old Fashion Aromatic Bitters, West Indian Orange Bitters, and their annual, limited-release Whiskey Barrel–Aged Bitters. It comes out each spring, and when it's gone it's gone (or gets drastically marked up by retailers). Peach remains one of their top sellers, and other bitters in production include lemon, celery, grapefruit, cranberry, plum, cherry, mint, and rhubarb. Joe says they'll continue to release new flavors, adding, "I've got a 'no one will go thirsty' policy in place."

The Bitter Truth (Munich, Germany)

In 2006, Munich bartenders Stephan Berg and Alexander Hauck joined together to create the bitters and spirits company The Bitter Truth. Berg was an avid collector of historical cocktail artifacts and was in possession of an impressive selection of both contemporary and vintage bitters, affording him the unique opportunity to sample bitters that hadn't been produced in decades. The Bitter Truth helped open the door to the current bitters revival when, in summer 2006, they released their Orange Bitters and Old Time Aromatic Bitters. They followed this with the first lemon bitters available on the commercial market, and a second aromatic variety, Jerry Thomas' Own Decanter Bitters, based on a historical recipe from the nineteenth-century celebrity bartender. The arrival of their award-winning Original Celery Bitters marked the availability of this historical bitters for the first time in decades, and prompted *Saveur* magazine to include it in the 2011 chefs' edition of "The *Saveur* 100." Other bitters in their lineup include grapefruit, chocolate, and a fruity and spicy New Orleans–style Creole Bitters.

Bittermens (Brooklyn, New York)

Avery and Janet Glasser have been making some of the most respected small-batch bitters on the market today, starting in New York, then in San Francisco and in Boston. The Glassers are now back in New York: they've set up a commercial kitchen in Red Hook, Brooklyn, where they produce their bitters in distinctive cobalt-blue bottles. They've even gotten into the bar business with Amor y Amargo, New York City's first bitters-centric drink destination.

THE CRAFT BITTERS ALLIANCE

The rise of small-batch bitters makers working out of their home kitchens and getting press on food blogs can be a bit of a bitter pill for some. Avery Glasser (who, with his wife, Janet, founded the popular Bittermens line of bitters) prides himself on having leapt every legal hurdle necessary to have his commercial bitters classified and sold as a nonpotable alcoholic product through the Alcohol and Tobacco Tax and Trade Bureau (TTB) and the Food and Drug Administration (FDA). He's been vocal about warning the newer bitters makers, who are technically unlicensed alcohol producers, that unless they go through all the steps necessary to get their products cleared by the TTB and FDA they risk having their business shut down. Any bars or restaurants using their bitters or retailers selling them could be fined as well. Learn more about the registration process at the Craft Bitters Alliance (www.craftbittersalliance.com).

Bittermens' amazing Xocolatl Mole and Hopped Grapefruit bitters announced their seriousness in bringing out inventive bitters, and newer flavors include a citrus-heavy Boston Bittahs, an island-spice 'Elemakule Tiki, and the tart and spicy Burlesque Bitters. Although they are no longer in regular production, keep an eye out for seasonal and limited-run favorites, such as Squirrel Nut, Moroccan Orange, and Pepper Cake, which are sometimes resurrected and put back into rotation.

In February 2009, Bittermens entered into a licensing agreement with Germany's The Bitter Truth, which allowed The Bitter Truth to produce and distribute cobranded versions of Bittermens' popular grapefruit and Xocolatl Mole bitters. Like most cocktail bitters, Bittermens bitters are classified as nonpotable by the Alcohol and Tobacco Tax and Trade Bureau, allowing them to be sold as nonbeverage alcohol (as vanilla extract is). But when The Bitter Truth entered the US market they elected to classify their products as potable alcohol, which meant that, depending on the state, you might be able to find Bitter Truth products only in liquor stores, and not in specialty shops or online sites selling bar supplies. Reacting to their—and their fans'—growing frustration with that limited distribution arrangement, in 2010 Bittermens decided to end their relationship with The Bitter Truth rather than sacrifice their relationship with consumers, who were used to finding Bittermens products outside liquor stores. The new arrangement seems to have benefited Bittermens, as those cobalt-blue bottles are now being distributed around the country.

It's an interesting scenario, since The Bitter Truth also produces a line of liqueurs in addition to their bitters. For them, it makes sense to classify their entire inventory as potable alcohol for ease of shipping their products into the United States. In New York, for example, you can legally buy The Bitter Truth only in a liquor store (where it's illegal to sell nonpotable bitters like Angostura or Fee Brothers). From a point of purchase perspective it makes sense—you're buying a bottle of Plymouth gin, so you might as well pick up a bottle of orange bitters while you're there—but it also keeps their brand from being sold with other bitters.

Dr. Adam Elmegirab's Bitters (Aberdeen, Scotland)
After mixing his way through every recipe in Jerry Thomas's *The Bartender's Guide: How to Mix Drinks or The Bon Vivant's Companion* and charting his progress on his blog, called The Jerry Thomas Project, Adam Elmegirab of Evo-Lution Bar Consultancy decided it was time to reintroduce Boker's Bitters to the market. First created in 1828, Boker's Bitters is called for in a number of vintage cocktail books, but Prohibition rendered it extinct. Consulting original tasting notes, a sample of the original Boker's, and an 1853 recipe, Elmegirab set to work to re-create this Golden Age bitters and market it to contemporary bars. Thanks to Adam you can now taste a historically accurate Martinez, crusta, or Japanese Cocktail. In 2009, Elmegirab followed his Boker's success with the creation of Dandelion & Burdock Bitters, modeled after a British beverage that was one of his favorites as a young man. He also produces a limited-edition Spanish Bitters, a citrus and chamomile formula based on recipes from the 1800s and 1900s.

A.B. Smeby Bittering Co. (Brooklyn, New York)
Louis Smeby, a waiter at The Modern in New York City, is creating some of the most inventive bitters coming out of Brooklyn, but they're also some of the most difficult to come by. Popularity sometimes yields distribution struggles with small-batch bitters makers, but while you're waiting for your own personal shipment you can sample these amazing bitters at a number of New York and Brooklyn restaurants and bars such as PDT and Buttermilk

Channel. Sourcing as many local products as possible and taking a seasonal approach to flavors, Smeby maintains a rotation of twenty different bitters, including Highland Heather (smoky and floral, with a base of single-malt scotch), Hibiscus Rose, Buddha's Hand Lemon–Kaffir Lime, Apple Cinnamon with Molasses, Lemon Verbena, Nasturtium-Cumin, Spice Cranberry, Clementine-Jasmine, Black and White (which tastes like the classic New York cookie of the same name), and a spicy Chai & Rye.

Scrappy's Bitters (Seattle, Washington)
Seattle bartender Miles "Scrappy" Thomas came out of the gate swinging in 2009 with his namesake bitters, which are made with many locally sourced ingredients. As soon as they were released they quickly found their way from Seattle's Tavern Law to New York's Death & Co. Scrappy's distinctive hand-numbered labels really stand out among the bitters bottles on the bar. His signature bitters is an aromatic lavender, but the cardamom remains a best seller that's hard to keep in stock. Other single-flavor products include celery, chocolate, orange, grapefruit, and lime, and there are also limited-release seasonal batches such as tangerine and apricot.

The Bitter Cube (Milwaukee, Wisconsin)
Nicholas Kosevich, an award-winning bartender, and Ira Koplowitz, who worked at Chicago's Violet Hour, are the two men behind The Bitter Cube. They use the Milwaukee restaurant Bacchus as their laboratory, turning out orange, cherry bark–vanilla, blackstrap, and Bolivar bitters (the last with floral notes sweetened with dried fruits and spiced with cinnamon), as well as two versions of Jamaican Bitters (one floral and fruity, the other warm and spicy). They also develop custom bitters blends for clients.

The Bitter End (Santa Fe, New Mexico)
Bill York rolled out his line of distinctly spicy Bitter End Bitters in 2010 with the goal of "giving standard bitters a radical twist." At times the heat in these threaten to overpower any cocktail they're added to. Their fun blends include Memphis (a smoky coffee-chipotle blend), Moroccan ("like a tagine in your cocktail glass"), Mexican Mole, Jamaican Jerk, and Thai.

Brooklyn Hemispherical Bitters (Brooklyn, New York)
In late 2010, Mark Buettler, the former head bartender at Dressler in Williamsburg, Brooklyn, teamed up with cocktail writer Jason Rowan to

found Brooklyn Hemispherical Bitters. Their signature Sriracha Bitters is a spicy bitters made with Dressler's homemade version of the popular hot sauce. Other seasonal flavors in rotation include strawberry, peach, Meyer lemon, blueberry, and black mission fig.

Bob's Bitters (London, England)
These single-flavor bitters, created by the mysterious "Bob" at The Bar at the Dorchester in London, come in flavors like cardamom, chocolate, ginger, grapefruit, lavender, licorice, peppermint, and vanilla.

Bar Keep Bitters (Monrovia, California)
At the 2009 Tales of the Cocktail in New Orleans, Tru Organic Spirits hosted a Barmade Bitters Challenge, looking for the best homemade bitters in three categories: fruit, herb, and spice. The winning certified all-organic bitters—Adam Seger's Swedish Herb, John Hogan and Tobin Ellis's Lavender Spice, and Marshall Altier's Baked Apple—are now available nationally through the Greenbar Collective under the name Bar Keep Bitters.

Urban Moonshine (Burlington, Vermont)
Launched in 2009 by herbalist Jovial King, Urban Moonshine is a small family business that focuses on bitters and tonics intended to supplement healthy, organic living but which also work wonders in a cocktail. Using organic grape alcohol and spring water, their original, citrus, and maple bitters come in 2-ounce dropper bottles, an 8.4-ounce flask, and a 10-milliliter spray bottle.

Sweetgrass (Union, Maine)

Along with a number of creative concoctions like cranberry gin, Maple Smash Liqueur, and peach wine, the Sweetgrass Farm Winery & Distillery in Union, Maine, also makes tart wine-based cranberry and blueberry bitters.

Bitters, Old Men (New York, New York)

In 2009, food writer Zachary Feldman lived every home bitters maker's dream: his homemade bourbon bitters debuted on the menu of Jim Meehan's PDT, in a drink called the Salted Chocolate Flip. Two years later, Feldman was running his own small-batch bitters business. From the cheeky logo to the slogan of "Get Bitt Slapped," Bitters, Old Men gets in your face with its message. Feldman's line-up includes flavors like roasted macadamia and papaya, along with themed bitters such as Great in '28, Smoke Gets in Your Bitters, Gangsta Lee'n, and Isaan Another Level bitters. They even make a restorative tonic, sold in a 1-ounce wax-capped glass bottle, that's meant to be knocked back in one pull, like Underberg.

Miracle Mile Bitters Co. (Los Angeles, California)

Former Miramax executive turned cocktail enthusiast Louis Anderman has been making quite a splash with his Miracle Mile bitters, whose labels are emblazoned with the words "Handcrafted in the Heart of Los Angeles." The chocolate/chili remains one of his most popular bitters, with batches of sour cherry, yuzu, fig, and gingerbread rounding out his ever-experimental list.

Bitter Tears (Los Angeles, California)

Created by a cocktail-loving couple from Highland Park who run a pop-up bar called Ms. and His, the Bitter Tears line is branded with whimsical titles. Lucille, with its blood orange and ginger, is a nod to a certain legendary comedic redhead, while Lolita packs top notes of sour cherry and vanilla for a balance of sweet and sour. And, naturally, a bitters named Ms. Piggy will hit you with a karate chop of smoky bacon rounded with peppercorn and serrano chile.

Snake Oil Bitters (Brooklyn, New York)

Not much is known about this lineup of Brooklyn bitters or their creator, but in addition to an aromatic original bitters, a lavender, and a chamomile, they make a one-of-a-kind tobacco bitters that introduces a spicy smokiness to any cocktail.

House Made Bitters (Victoria, British Columbia)

These small-batch bitters and syrups are currently available only in Canada. Their lineup includes grapefruit, lavender, cherry, chocolate, and apricot bitters.

Stirrings (New Bedford, Massachusetts)

Stirrings, which produces a line of cocktail mixers, syrups, and flavored sugars for rimming glasses, also makes a blood orange bitters in an oversized 12-ounce bottle. They were the first, and are still one of the only, producers to offer a commercial blood orange bitters, but be aware that it isn't made with alcohol. Aside from the preservation factor—you'll have to keep these refrigerated once opened—they're a bit too sweet and not concentrated enough to achieve the same results as traditional cocktail bitters.

Cocktail Kingdom (New York, New York)

In 2010 Greg Boehm of Cocktail Kingdom and Mud Puddle Books introduced Cocktail Kingdom Wormwood Bitters. Formulated by the cofounder of the blog Scofflaw's Den, SeanMike Whipkey, they are bottled at Berkshire Mountain Distillers.

Boudreau's Bitters (Seattle, Washington)

Jamie Boudreau, the inventive Canadian bartender who now calls Seattle home, has teased bitters lovers with the promise of making his popular homemade bitters available to consumers (there's even a website and Facebook page displaying the ornate labels). I've sampled both his cherry and Boker's bitters (which Boudreau reverse-engineered after tasting a sample of the original), and they're outstanding. At the time of this writing, Boudreau was still working on finalizing production. I just wish I had hit him up for more sample bottles before I left Seattle.

Amargo Chuncho Bitters (Peru)

You'll find this decorative bottle of bitters popping up more and more these days. Their primary application is in Peru's national drink, the pisco sour.

Hermes Bitters (Japan)

Be warned, the quest to find Hermes Bitters outside of Japan can lead to disappointment (or late-night online auctions). Created by Suntory, Hermes Orange Bitters and Hermes Original Aromatic Bitters are the holy grail for bitters lovers, both because anything that's impossible to find inspires devotion, and because the orange bitters are some of the best out there. In the past, if you had a contact in Japan you could arrange to have some bottles sent your way, but, unfortunately, Suntory stopped production on them. So if you see a bar with Hermes bitters in stock, ask for them.

WHERE TO BUY BITTERS

Whether it's born out of necessity, inspired by the economy, or is simply an attempt to reconnect with an artisanal craftsmanship, the same DIY spirit inherent in making your own pickles, jams, cheese, and chocolate bars extends to small-batch bitters. Brooklyn, in particular, has been the setting for much of the bitters renaissance. *New York Times* restaurant critic Sam Sifton crafted an amusing description of Brooklyn's bitters scene in his two-star review of Prime Meats in Carroll Gardens: "Have a Manhattan made by one of the whiz kids back behind the bar, some mustachioed chemist with tattoos and an understanding of bitters that rivals a rabbi's knowledge of the Talmud. The staff is exceptionally well trained and efficient, a crew of handsome men and women dressed as if ready to ride horses back home to Bushwick, where they trap beaver and make their own candles."

But even though new commercial, small-batch, and individual bitters makers seem to appear every month, making bitters a buzzword among bartenders and cocktail enthusiasts, bitters are still a decidedly niche sector of the cocktail and spirits market. And despite their newfound popularity, locating bitters can still be a challenge.

The Internet has increased awareness of bitters and their role in cocktails, in addition to giving people the ability to locate, share, and talk about bitters from all around the world. Bitters makers, whether as big as Angostura or just a one-man basement operation, all have websites. The best sites offer a list of available bitters, have descriptions with tasting notes, and, most important, indicate where customers can buy the product. Ideally, the website will also offer useful information such as a list of bars where you can sample the bitters, links to specialty retailers who carry them, and sample recipes.

The most fervent collectors of bitters often turn to online auction sites. Although you can find many old bitters bottles at reasonable prices, tracking down a vintage bottle of a lost bitters is an extremely competitive (and expensive) sport. Stephan Berg and Alexander Hauck, founders of The Bitter Truth, note that in each auction you're actually bidding against three different parties: glass collectors, label collectors, and cocktail enthusiasts. The last group in particular will pay plenty for a bitters bottle, especially if there's a chance that one last drop or a little debris remains there to sample.

If you're wondering about a specific bitters—whether you want to know where to buy it or how to use it—Google is your best friend. A simple online search will lead you down a bitters-soaked rabbit hole of cocktail forums, discussion boards, and blogs filled with a spirited exchange of useful information.

That said, there are a few reliable online retailers that sell many hard-to-find products: Cocktail Kingdom (www.cocktailkingdom.com) and The Boston Shaker (www.thebostonshaker.com) have been my go-to online outlets to pick up new bitters, especially those from smaller producers. KegWorks, through their own site (www.kegworks.com) and via Amazon, carries Angostura, Peychaud's, Regans' Orange Bitters No. 6, Fee Brothers, Urban Moonshine, and Bitter End, among others. DrinkUpNY (www.drinkupny.com), the online operation for Brooklyn's Borisal Liquor & Wine, carries the full line of Bitter Truth products.

Not every city is blessed with a bitters emporium, so if you find one near you, frequent it and support it to keep the bitters flowing. Some great spots to scoop up some bitters include DeLaurenti Specialty Food & Wine (Seattle), The Meadow (Portland, New York), Cask (San Francisco), Bar Keeper (Los Angeles), The Boston Shaker (Boston), Kalustyan's (New York), Ace Beverage (Washington, D.C.), and Pearl Specialty Market & Spirits (Portland). And keep an eye out for bitters in provisions stores and markets. In my neighborhood in Brooklyn, it seems like every upscale grocer has a handful of Fee Brothers bitters on the shelf, and restaurants like Marlow & Sons sell their own house-made bitters.

For more on locations where you can purchase bitters, both online and at brick-and-mortar stores, see the Resources section on page 220.

TASTING BITTERS

During a weekend on the bitters trail in San Francisco, I hit up a number of bars and restaurants, and at each one I'd ask if they made their own bitters and, if so, could I have a taste? Some places just handed me the bottle to do with as I pleased. Was I expected to take a chug from the bottle? Apply it to my finger to taste? One bartender yanked my hand across the bar and sprinkled a drop on its back to lick off like the salt for a tequila shooter, and at Nopa they presented me with a tasting flight of their many house-made bitters in tiny plastic cups.

At The Meadow, a wonderfully quirky bicoastal boutique in Portland and Manhattan that specializes in finishing salts, chocolate, flowers, and bitters, customers can dip a toothpick into any of their sample bottles of bitters to give them a try. Another way to taste is to simply put a drop on your finger and give it a lick. You'll pick up the primary flavor component, but you'll also sense the heat from the alcohol, which can instantly over-power the more subtle flavors. Keep in mind that aromatic bitters aren't meant to be potable on their own; they're intended to be applied to a drink.

When I'm tasting bitters I haven't tried before, or if I'm considering how to use a particular type of bitters in a drink, I like to start with my nose. I drop a dash in my palm and take a look at its viscosity. Whether it runs all over the place or holds its shape can tip you off to the quality of the base spirit used (you want the drops to have some structure). Then rub your hands together to "warm up" the bitters. Cup your hands together, bring them to your nose, and inhale to take in the aromatics. This will help you pick up some of the individual notes at play, whether they are cinnamon, cardamom, clove, hops, or orange peel. This should then get you thinking about which spirits would play well with the bitters. Jim Meehan of PDT describes it as "picking a team"—"What players are you going to put out on the floor who are going to play well with this guy?"

After that, I like to taste the bitters by diluting two dashes in a shot glass of club soda or seltzer. Ultimately, however, the best way to taste bitters is to test them out in a cocktail. A gin martini is a great vehicle to experiment with citrus, herbal, or floral bitters, while a Manhattan serves as a great base for aromatic bitters. Keep in mind that rather than building a drink around bitters, you should use the bitters to complement a cocktail. They should play a supporting role that's so subtle you might not even know they're there. And, as in any delicious cocktail, the final product should be greater than the sum of its parts.

USING BITTERS

What constitutes a dash of bitters can vary by brand, depending on the type of bottle and, more importantly, the size of the dasher cap. That's why some bartenders, like those at Momofuku Ssäm Bar, decant their store-bought bitters into uniform vessels to ensure a dash is the same no matter the brand.

Unless you're using a dropper to skillfully deposit a drop on a pisco sour (page 143), there's no need to be bashful with your dash. Flip the bottle right over and shake it over the drink, like you're doctoring up a lunchtime burrito with hot sauce. If a recipe calls for a dash and the bottle you're using barely gives up a sprinkle, then give it another shake or two as needed. If you're using a bitters bottle with a dropper instead of a dasher cap, four to five drops should equal a dash. Usually bitters are added to the shaker while you're building your drink, but sometimes, especially when they are employed for their aromatics, bitters can be added to the top of a finished drink or even sprayed across the surface using an atomizer.

A Saturation of Bitters?

Considering the scarcity of bitters less than a decade ago, it seems impolite to even raise the question, but are there too many bitters out there now? While having a host of orange bitters to choose from offers room to experiment, how many lavender bitters does one really need? It does seem that nearly every possible fruit has been zested, every exotic herb dried and infused. Celery bitters has proven that there is a lot of potential for vegetable bitters, but how much is too much? Cocktailian Dale DeGroff says, "If they can make them and there is a market, why not? It happened that way in the nineteenth century: there were many proprietary bitters, and I am glad to see it happening again. Too many? Well, the market will decide that question."

Admittedly, even for a bitters geek like myself, just keeping up with the new bitters popping up on my Google Alerts every morning makes my head spin. David Wondrich's thoughts on the matter: "I'm amused by it. I haven't tried them all, needless to say (how could one), but I assume they follow the standard bell curve in quality. Eventually things will calm down and we'll have a reasonable number to deal with."

Robert Hess, who was obsessing over bitters long before the current rainbow of flavors became available, says, "I personally think the world can use only so many new bitters. Once you get beyond a handful of them, you end up just having different bitters for the sake of having different bitters. I'm just thankful that the overall craft of the cocktail has improved enough so that folks know that there *are* bitters other than Angostura out there, even if they may not have access to them."

A pragmatic Jim Meehan continues in that vein. He says, "I've come to the realization that my bartop has so many bottles that it's hard to reach over bottles to serve someone their drink or a hot dog. These bitters bottles often stand in the way of me and my guest talking about anything other than bitters." He's also concerned about the longevity of many of these new bitters, saying, "My goal is to make drinks that will be around twenty years from now. Looking at all of these bitters . . . Angostura, Fee Brothers, Peychaud's are the only ones I can be confident will be around twenty years from now."

Dandelion Botanical Co.
WILD CLUB
WILD
(206) 545 8892 dandelionbotanical.com

Dandelion Botanical Co.
WILD CHERRY BARK
WILD
(206) 545-8892 dandelionbotanical.com

Dandelion Botanical Co.
SCHIZANDRA BERRIES
ORGANIC
(206) 545-8892 dandelionbotanical.com

Dandelion Botanical Co.
GENTIANA LUTEUM
ORGANIC
(206) 545 8892 dandelionbotanical.com

MAKING
YOUR OWN
BITTERS

You started with a bottle of Angostura and you've just added an orange bitters and a couple of small-batch bitters you tracked down online to your collection. So why would you want to make your own bitters? For the same reason people make their own homebrew, or spend an entire weekend canning and preserving—for the unabashed pride of making something with your own hands. (Not to mention the fact that small-batch artisanal bitters can cost north of twenty dollars a bottle.) How many of your friends are making their own bitters? Aside from the esoteric (read: cool) factor, creating your own gives you the freedom to experiment with signature flavors and to take advantage of seasonal ingredients. Right after Christmas citrus is at its peak. Break out your paring knife and zester and start peeling all of those gorgeous clementines, tangerines, satsumas, and blood oranges. When spring blooms, get to work on some tart rhubarb bitters. Summer berries make delicious bitters. And when autumn rolls around, scoop up Concord grapes, husk cherries, apples, and pears. Whenever I see an exotic piece of fruit at the market, my first thought is, "This might make a decent bitters."

There are two basic methods to making bitters: you can build a custom bitters by mixing together preinfused tinctures to taste, or you can add all of the ingredients into one vessel and infuse them together. Creating a batch of bitters by blending various single-flavor tinctures affords you better control of each element that goes into the mix, but the small-batch, one-pot method is a great starting point for making your own bitters.

A hybrid method to consider—something I picked up from my friend Maggie (see her recipe for rhubarb bitters on page 68)—is to secure the bittering agents in disposable tea bags. Since each ingredient infuses at a different rate, you can pull out the bags one by one whenever you like while you allow the other ingredients to continue steeping.

What is a tincture? A tincture is a single-flavor infusion (whereas bitters are a combination of many flavors). Another difference between tinctures and bitters is that bitters are often diluted with water or slightly sweetened with burnt sugar, honey, or simple syrup, while tinctures remain concentrated at a high proof. The alcohol content for most bitters will be around 45 percent alcohol, or 90 proof. Tinctures can have an alcohol content of 60 to 120 proof or higher.

Making tinctures is very simple: fill a glass jar a quarter of the way with whatever ingredient you are using—orange peel, rosemary, cocoa nibs, cinnamon, gentian root, raspberries—and fill with a high-proof spirit until it covers the solids. Your solids to liquid ratio will vary: it's typically

3:1 or 4:1 alcohol to solid, but the key is to make sure the solid matter is completely covered with alcohol. With tinctures, I generally stick with Everclear or a high-proof vodka to maintain a neutral flavor, but if you are working with something like vanilla or cinnamon, you can try using a more flavor-forward bourbon, rye, or rum.

Tinctures can take anywhere from a day or two to a couple of weeks to achieve their desired flavor, although some herbal tinctures are ready in just a few hours. When you're working with a single ingredient, you can easily use visual cues like color changes in the solution to monitor the progress as the alcohol takes on the color of the primary ingredient. In addition to being used as building blocks for bitters, tinctures can be introduced to a cocktail by way of a single drop or a spritz from an atomizer on the surface of the drink for an aromatic garnish.

The recipes that follow serve as an introduction to making your own bitters, but once you've made a basic bitters I encourage you to experiment with tinctures, too. Ultimately, mixing single-ingredient tinctures is the best way to learn how each ingredient should taste when properly infused, and it will allow you to control the final product when making bitters.

BITTERS BASICS

The botanicals used to make bitters are fairly inexpensive but, unless you have a neighborhood herbalist, you'll likely need to order some of the harder-to-find items online. When I lived in Seattle I was extremely fortunate to have access to Tenzing Momo, a Tibetan apothecary located in the heart of Pike Place Market. Tenzing Momo sells its wares online, but there's a touch of magic about the aromatic shop, which is stocked with tarot cards, bulk tea, and essential oils, and where you can ask the shopkeeper questions as he measures out aromatic herbs and botanicals. Seattle bitters makers are also lucky to have easy access to the Dandelion Botanical Company. In New York I purchase my bitters-making botanicals primarily at Kalustyan's, a kaleidoscopic culinary outpost on Lexington at 28th Street that's bursting with more than four thousand different herbs, teas, and spices. If you're not lucky enough to have access to one of these shops, see the Resources section (page 220) for information about other shops and online retailers where you can find the items you need.

Botanicals, Herbs, and Spices

Below is a list of some dried herbs, spices, and botanicals that are often used for making bitters. The recipes that follow don't include every one of these, but this should serve as a shopping list to help stock your bitters-making kit.

BITTERING AGENTS

Angelica root
Barberry root bark
Birch leaf
Black walnut leaf
Burdock root
Calamus root
Chirayata
Cinchona bark (a.k.a.
    Peruvian bark)
Dandelion bark/
    dandelion leaf
Devil's club root (a.k.a.
    devil's walking stick)
Fringe tree bark
Gentian root
Horehound
Licorice root
Orris root
Quassia chips
Wild cherry bark
Wormwood

FLAVOR AGENTS

Arnica flowers
Allspice berries
Anise seed
Caraway seed
Cardamom pods (green)
Cassia chips
Cinnamon
Citrus peel (orange, grapefruit,
    lemon, lime)
Clove
Coriander seeds
Fennel seeds
Grains of paradise
Hibiscus flowers
Hops
Hyssop
Juniper berries
Lavender
Lemongrass
Milk thistle
Nutmeg
Peppermint
Rose hips
Sarsaparilla
Sassafras
Schizandra berries
Star anise

Bittering Agents

These are the herbs, roots, barks, and botanicals that will provide much of the actual bitterness to your brew—ingredients like gentian, quassia, cinchona bark, fringe tree bark, cherry root bark, and calamus root. Use roots or other solid ingredients instead of powders, since powders are much more difficult to strain from the solution. Barks and roots will also introduce a natural woody taste to the solution.

Flavor Agents

These ingredients (or ingredient, if you opt to use only one) will be responsible for your primary flavor profile, whether it's citrus, coffee, nuts, herbs, fruit, or flowers. With fruits, herbs, and flowers, I like to use a combination of fresh and dried ingredients to increase the complexity of the flavor. Your fresh ingredients should be as fresh as possible. Use organic fruit when it's available, and be sure to wash the fruit thoroughly since you'll primarily be using the skins and peels.

A NOTE ON CITRUS ZEST

Unless otherwise noted, when a recipe calls for citrus zest, cut large strips of zest from the fruit with a paring knife or vegetable peeler. Try to take the zest only and little to none of the white pith, which can be overwhelmingly bitter.

Spirit Solution

Your biggest investment in making bitters will be the spirits necessary to make the infusions. Using high-proof or overproof spirits speeds up the infusion process because they extract more flavor from the solid ingredients over a shorter period of time. High-proof spirits also act as a preservative, allowing the bitters to remain shelf stable long after you've opened them.

Depending on where you live, you may not be able to easily find grain alcohol like Everclear. If that's the case, use a high-proof or overproof vodka (at least 90 proof, which means it is 45 percent alcohol), but don't skimp here: rotgut vodka will not yield the best results. If you're using bourbon,

Dried Citrus Peels

Dried fruit peel adds both a concentrated citrus flavor and a natural bitterness to your homemade bitters. You can usually find dried orange peel in health food stores and herb shops, but it only takes a bowlful of fresh fruit and some patience (which you already have if you're investing the time to turn out your own bitters) to make your own. If you have a few days, you can air-dry your peels by leaving them spread out on a baking sheet; alternatively, you can dry them more quickly in a low oven. The basic method below can be used to dry any type of citrus peel.

Makes ¹/₂ cup

*3 grapefruit,
8 lemons, 8 limes,
or 6 oranges*

Preheat the oven to 200°F. Wash and dry the fruit. Peel off the zest in long strips using a zester or paring knife. Finely chop the zest strips. Spread the chopped zest on a baking sheet and put it in the oven until dried, at least 30 minutes. Store in an airtight container.

rye, tequila, or rum, use the best-quality, highest-proof brand you can find. For most of these recipes I used grain alcohol, Absolut 100 vodka, Wild Turkey 101-proof rye and bourbon, or Gosling's 151-proof rum.

BITTERS-MAKING GEAR

See Basic Bar Tools (page 80) for more information on some of the tools listed below and a list of additional gear you'll need for mixing drinks.

Knives, Zesters, Peelers

You'll need a chef's knife and a paring knife for cutting fruit and chopping herbs. You can use a paring knife or a swivel peeler (also known as a vegetable peeler) for removing the zest from fruit, or use a Microplane grater when you want finely grated zest.

Cutting Board

A large hardwood or nonporous polyethylene cutting board is necessary for prep work.

Mortar and Pestle

This isn't a must-have—you can always crack seeds and spices using the flat side of a chef's knife—but a heavy mortar and pestle is great to have on hand. I picked up a fifteen-pound granite number when I was in graduate school and it's still going strong. Plus, it comes in handy when making guacamole.

Mason Jars

I find that wide-mouth, quart-sized Mason jars work best, but you can use any large glass vessel with a lid. These are pretty affordable by the case at grocery or hardware stores, especially in the summer, during the height of canning and preserving season. Unlike when you're canning, though, you don't need to sterilize the jars before using them (the high-proof alcohol should do the trick), but make sure they're washed with hot water or run through a dishwasher before you use them. I also use wide-mouth pint and half-pint Mason jars to store many of the aromatics, seeds, and botanicals I use for making bitters.

Cheesecloth

You will need a lot of cheesecloth, so stock up. I like to use the 100 percent cotton Regency brand. Some home bitters makers swear by coffee filters, but the time it takes to strain liquid through them is too long for my taste. And though some use a Brita water filter for straining, I think it's too much work for the end results.

Funnels

You'll need two: one average-sized funnel for straining from jar to jar, and a small one for decanting bitters into bottles.

Bottles

Once your beautiful bitters are ready for service, you'll want to transfer them from their Mason jars to smaller bottles. You can find an assortment of glass bottles at retailers like The Container Store, but I'd stay away from bottles with corks or hinged lids. Ultimately, you'll want to cap your bottles with a built-in dropper, dripper insert, or woozy cap (the plastic snap-on lid with a hole in it, like you see on a soy sauce or hot sauce bottle). I order most of my bottles from Specialty Bottle in Seattle. You can get 5-ounce clear glass bottles with woozy caps starting at about 60 cents, 2-ounce amber bottles with droppers for about 70 cents, and 2-ounce cobalt glass bottles with droppers for about a dollar.

Labels

While my bitters are infusing I use blue painter's tape and a Sharpie to label and date each jar. Once you decant the bitters, you'll want to use a label maker to clearly label each jar, or, if you're going to present it to someone, you can go the extra step and make custom labels using stickers or labels from a stationery store. Or let your inner graphic designer loose and go to town with Photoshop to make professional-looking labels.

BITTERS EXCHANGE

If you run with a group of bitters-loving friends, why not host a party at which you make bitters together as a group? This saves some labor on all of the peeling, chopping, and zesting, and you can combine resources to gather the spirits you need. Try organizing the event around a particular theme; everyone can make his or her own twist on one basic type of bitters, like orange bitters, for example. At the end of the night everyone takes their jar home with them. Then regroup a month later with a sample-size bottle for everyone to taste and test in cocktails.

HOMEMADE BITTERS

All of the following recipes will take you at least a month to make from start to finish. Patience is key. As a wise Floridian once said (well, sang), the waiting is the hardest part.

KALUSTYAN'S
SINCE 1944
A LANDMARK FOR FINE SPECIALTY FOODS

GREEN CARDAMOM PODS

(ELETTARIA CARDAMOMUM)
HAIL--MIDEAST/ ELAICHI--INDIA
IT HAS A PUNGENT AROMA AND A WARM SPICY-SWEET FLAVOR.

COMMONLY USED IN INDIAN SWEETS AND CURRIES, MID EAST DESSERTS AND COFFEE, EUROPEAN BAKED GOODS. SEEDS CAN BE CHEWED AS BREATH FRESHNER

$16.99 SPS827 **7 OZ**

123 LEXINGTON AVE., N.Y., N.Y. 10016
Phone: 212-685-3451 Fax: 212-683-8458

$12.99

KALUSTYAN'S
SINCE 1944

CORRIANDER SEED

CORIANDERUM SATNUM
DHANIA--INDIA
HAS STRONG NUTTY AROMA AND SWEETISH PIQUANT TASTE. GROUND CORIANDER ACTS AS A THICKENER IN SAUCES & GRAVIES, AND IN CURRIES.
MUST BE SLOWLY DRY ROAST BEFORE GRINDING OR CRUSHING.

$4.99 SPS868 **7 OZ.**

123 LEXINGTON AVE., N.Y., N.Y. 10016
Phone: 212-685-3451 Fax: 212-683-8458

GREEN CARDAMON PODS	CA...	INDIAN CORRIANDER SEED
SPS827 7oz	SPS82...	SPS868 7oz

KALUSTYAN'S
SINCE 1944
A LANDMARK FOR FINE SPECIALTY FOODS

GRAINS OF PARADISE

GUINEA / MELEGUETA PEPPER
THESE SEEDS HAVE MANY MEDICAL AS WELL AS **CULINARY USES.**
THEY ARE BITING ON TONGUE, LIKE BLACK PEPPER, BUT GRINDING RELEASES THEIR SWEET AROMA AND WHITE INTERIOR. MOST FAMOUS BRAZILIAN DISH FEIJOADA REQUIRES GRAINS OF PARADISE FOR HOT LITTLE CHILI.

$9.99 SPS4444 **3 oz**

123 LEXINGTON AVE., N.Y., N.Y. 10016
Phone: 212-685-3451 Fax: 212-683-8458

GRAINS OF PARADISE
GUINEA / MEL...

$3.99 S861 **3 oz**

KALUSTYAN'S
SINCE 1944
A LANDMARK FOR FINE SPECIALTY FOODS

WHOLE CLOVE

SYZYGIUM AOMATICUM
LAUNG--INDIA
GHARANFUL--MIDEAST
USED IN BOTH SAVOURY AND SWEET DISHES. ALSO USED IN SPICED TEA.
IT HAS SHARP, PUNGENT TASTE & FRAGRANT AROMA.

...RAINS OF ...RADISE	GRAINS OF PARADISE	...VE	WHOLE CLOVE

KALUSTYAN'S
SINCE 1944
A LANDMARK FOR FINE SPECIALTY FOODS

LUCKNOW FENNEL

LAKHNAWI SAUNF
IT IS SMALLER, THINNER, MORE FINELY TEXTURED, AND HAS A MORE DELICATE FLAVOR THAN FENNEL SEEDS.
THIS IS THE VARIETY OF FENNEL WHICH IS TRADITIONALLY SERVED AS AFTER DINNER. AROMA IS GREATLY ENHANCED WHEN DRY ROASTED.
USED ALSO IN COOKING AS REGULR FENNEL.

$5.99 SPS033 **7 oz**

123 LEXINGTON AVE., N.Y., N.Y. 10016
Phone: 212-685-3451 Fax: 212-683-8458

$3.99

KALUSTYAN'S
SINCE 1944
A LANDMARK FOR FINE SPECIALTY FOODS

WHOLE NUTMEG

(JAIFAL)

$12.99 **14oz**

SPS952

123 LEXINGTON AVE., N.Y., N.Y. 10016
Phone: 212-685-3451 Fax: 212-683-845...

FENNEL SEED (SAUNF)	FEN... SE... (SAU...	WHOLE NUTMEG (JAIFAL)

KALUSTYAN'S SINCE 1944 A LANDMARK FOR FINE SPECIALTY FOODS

WHOLE ALL SPICE
JAMAICA PEPPER
BAHAR--MIDEAST
$9.99

ALL SPICE
(JAMAICA PEPPER)
SPS8081   14oz

WHOLE ALL SPICE
(JAMAICA PE
SPS808

$6.99

ANISE SEED
ANISE HAS A DISTINCTIVE SWEET LICIRICE FLAVOR. IT PERFUMES AND FLAVORS A VARIETY OF CONFECTIONS AS WELL AS SAVORY DISHES. IT IS ALSO USED TO FLAVOR DRINKS SUCH AS ARRAK OR OUZO ETC.CANDIED TO BE USED AS MOUTH FRESHNER.
$6.99   7 OZ
123 LEXINGTON AVE., N.Y., N.Y. 10016
Phone: 212-685-3451 Fax: 212-685-8458

ANISE SEED
SPS812   7oz

KALUSTYAN'S SINCE 1944 A LANDMARK FOR FINE SPECIALTY FOODS

NATURAL ORRIS ROOT
IRI X GERMANICA VAR. FLORENTIN
* PROVIDE BITTER FLAVORING.
* IT IS POWERFUL PURGATIVE BUT CONSULT PHYSICIAN FIRST.
* CAN BE CHEWED FOR DISAGREEBLE BREATH.
* USE AS TEA FOR COUGH ,HOARSENNESS. BRONCHITIS & COLIC.
* NOT FDA APPROVED.
$3.99   SPS738   2 OZ

ORRIS ROOT

KALUSTYAN'S S'NCE 1944 A LANDMARK FOR FINE SPECIALTY FOODS

MILK THISTLE
SEED / WHOLE
SILYBUM NARIANUM
C/S ORGANIC
SUPPORT FOR HEALTHY LIVER FUNCTION.
USED PARTICULARLY FOR TREATMENT OF LIVER RELATED DISORDERS. PROTECTS LIVER FROM TOXINS & HELP CLEAR PSORIASIS.
* NOT FDA APPROVED.
USE AS TEA WITH HONEY OR SUGAR
$2.99

MILK THISTLE
SEED/WHOLE
SPS709   1oz

KALUSTYAN'S SINCE 1944 A LANDMARK FOR FINE SPECIALTY FOODS

CEYLON CINNAMON M-4 STICKS
ALSO KNOWN AS "CANELA"
MEXICAN CINNAMON
A POPULAR SPICE FOR BOTH SAVOURY & SWEET DISHES.
$6.99   SPS2078   3 oz.
123 LEXINGTON AVE., N.Y., N.Y. 10016
Phone: 212-685-3451 Fax: 212-683-8458

CEYLON CINNAMON M-4 STICKS

KALUSTYAN'S SINCE A LANDMARK FINE SPECIALTY FOODS

DRIED ORANGE PEEL
$5.99   2oz

DRIED ORANGE PEEL
STRIPS
SPS1035   2oz

Apple Bitters

Makes about 20 ounces

Peels from 6 medium to large apples, preferably organic

Zest of ½ lemon, cut into strips with a paring knife

2 cinnamon sticks

½ teaspoon allspice berries

¼ teaspoon coriander seeds

½ teaspoon cassia chips

½ teaspoon cinchona bark

4 cloves

2 cups high-proof bourbon, or more as needed

1 cup water

2 tablespoons rich syrup (page 92)

There's no better sign that fall has arrived than a basket of crisp apples on the kitchen counter. Whether you pluck them straight off the tree at an orchard or pick them up from a vendor at the farmers' market, it's hard to resist eating them out of hand, but try to save a few for this recipe. The cinnamon and brown sugar echo the flavor of traditional apple pie, but in this recipe you use only the skin of the apples, a tip I picked up from Bobby Heugel at Houston's Anvil Bar (the peel introduces bitterness and apple flavor without the added sugar and water that would make the solution too sweet). This bitters adds a sweet spiciness to bourbon, rye, whiskey, applejack, or apple brandy, and is also just dandy in an old-fashioned or Manhattan.

Place all of the ingredients except for the bourbon, water, and rich syrup in a quart-sized Mason jar or other large glass container with a lid. Pour in the 2 cups of bourbon, adding more if necessary so that all the ingredients are covered. Seal the jar and store at room temperature out of direct sunlight for 2 weeks, shaking the jar once a day.

After 2 weeks, strain the liquid through a cheesecloth-lined funnel into a clean quart-sized jar to remove the solids. Repeat until all of the sediment has been filtered out. Squeeze the cheesecloth over the jar to release any excess liquid and transfer the solids to a small saucepan. Cover the jar and set aside.

Cover the solids in the saucepan with the water and bring to a boil over medium-high heat. Cover the saucepan, lower the heat, and simmer for 10 minutes.

Remove the saucepan from the heat and let cool completely. Once cooled, add the contents of the saucepan (both liquid and solids) to another quart-sized Mason jar. Cover the jar and store at room temperature out of direct sunlight for 1 week, shaking the jar daily.

After 1 week, strain the jar with the liquid and solids through a cheesecloth-lined funnel into a clean quart-sized Mason jar. Repeat until all of the sediment has been filtered out. Discard the solids. Add this liquid to the jar containing the original bourbon solution.

Add the rich syrup to the jar and stir to incorporate, then cover and shake to fully dissolve the syrup.

Allow the mixture to stand at room temperature for 3 days. At the end of the 3 days, skim off any debris that floats to the surface and pour the mixture through a cheesecloth-lined funnel one last time to remove any solids.

Using a funnel, decant the bitters into smaller jars and label. If there's any sediment left in the bottles, or if the liquid is cloudy, give the bottle a shake before using. The bitters will last indefinitely, but for optimum flavor use within a year.

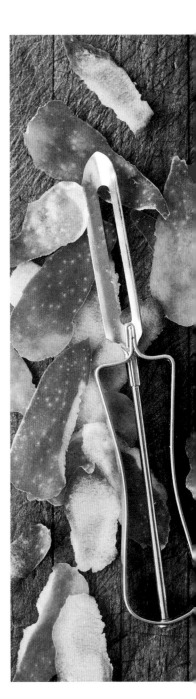

BTP House Bitters

Makes about 20 ounces

_____

2 tablespoons chopped dried
orange peel (page 47)

Zest of 1 orange, cut into
strips with a paring knife

¹/₄ cup dried sour cherries

5 green cardamom pods,
cracked

2 cinnamon sticks

1 star anise

1 vanilla bean, halved
lengthwise and seeds
scraped out (use both
pod and seeds)

¹/₄ teaspoon cloves

¹/₄ teaspoon quassia chips

¹/₄ teaspoon gentian root

¹/₂ teaspoon cassia chips

Pinch of dried black walnut
leaf

2 cups high-proof rye, or
more as needed

1 cup water

2 tablespoons rich syrup
(page 92)

A bottle of Angostura is an essential item to have in your liquor cabinet, but following this recipe to make your own signature "house bitters" is a creative DIY way to add another aromatic bitters to your collection. In this recipe you'll find the classic aromatics of cinnamon, cardamom, and clove rounded out with some sweetness from dried cherries and vanilla, and the bitters finishes with a burst of citrus from both dried and fresh orange peel. This basic recipe lends itself to improvisation; you can tweak it any way you like and bottle your own bespoke bitters. Use this wherever you would an aromatic bitters like Angostura.

_____

Place all of the ingredients except for the rye, water, and rich syrup in a quart-sized Mason jar or other large glass container with a lid. Pour in the 2 cups of rye, adding more if necessary so that all the ingredients are covered. Seal the jar and store at room temperature out of direct sunlight for 2 weeks, shaking the jar once a day.

After 2 weeks, strain the liquid through a cheesecloth-lined funnel into a clean quart-sized jar to remove the solids. Repeat until all of the sediment has been filtered out. Squeeze the cheesecloth over the jar to release any excess liquid and transfer the solids to a small saucepan. Cover the jar and set aside.

Cover the solids in the saucepan with the water and bring to a boil over medium-high heat. Cover the saucepan, lower the heat, and simmer for 10 minutes.

Remove the saucepan from the heat and let cool completely. Once cooled, add the contents of the saucepan (both liquid and solids) to another quart-sized Mason jar. Cover the jar and store at room temperature out of direct sunlight for 1 week, shaking the jar daily.

After 1 week, strain the jar with the liquid and solids through a cheesecloth-lined funnel into a clean quart-sized Mason jar. Repeat until all of the sediment has been filtered out. Discard the solids. Add this liquid to the jar containing the original rye solution.

Add the rich syrup to the jar and stir to incorporate, then cover and shake to fully dissolve the syrup.

Allow the mixture to stand at room temperature for 3 days. At the end of the 3 days, skim off any debris that floats to the surface and pour the mixture through a cheesecloth-lined funnel one last time to remove any solids.

Using a funnel, decant the bitters into smaller jars and label. If there's any sediment left in the bottles, or if the liquid is cloudy, give the bottle a shake before using. The bitters will last indefinitely, but for optimum flavor use within a year.

Charred Cedar Bitters

Makes about 20 ounces

---

*2 food-safe cedar sheets
(about 6 by 8 inches each)*

¼ teaspoon cinchona bark

¼ teaspoon wild cherry bark

¼ teaspoon cassia chips

*2 cups 101-proof bourbon, or
more as needed*

1 cup water

This bitters offers a bit of a cheat in achieving an authentic charred flavor. While aging homemade bitters in an actual whiskey barrel is ideal, it isn't always practical. It's getting easier to get your hands on used barrels from whiskey distillers (Hudson Valley's Tuthilltown Spirits is a great source for these), but even the smallest barrels hold around three gallons—and that's a lot of bitters. Mark Fuller, the chef and co-owner of West Seattle's restaurant Spring Hill, turned me on to soaking pieces of charred food-safe cedar sheets in your bitters solution to easily introduce a woody char. (Available on Amazon and at many cookware stores, these cedar sheets are about ⅛ inch thick and have the same pliability as balsa wood.) Beyond the cedar tip, I could never get Mark to share his actual recipe with me—he brushed it off as too simple to share—so I've done my best to replicate it with minimal ingredients. This bitters is fantastic with bourbon—but, then, it's hard to think of an aromatic bitters that isn't. At Spring Hill they serve it in their signature Gold 'n' Brown, a blend of Maker's Mark, bitters, and dry ginger ale. I don't add a sweetener to this one to let the char flavor really come through.

Place a cedar sheet on a baking sheet and, using a small kitchen torch, carefully run the flame back and forth across the cedar, completely charring the surface. Flip over and repeat on the opposite side. Repeat with the second cedar sheet. Once they have cooled, using kitchen scissors, cut them into squares about 3 by 3 inches and place in a quart-sized Mason jar or other large glass container with a lid.

Add all of the remaining ingredients to the jar except the bourbon and water. Pour in the 2 cups of bourbon, adding more if necessary so that all the ingredients are covered. Seal the jar and store at room temperature out of direct sunlight for 2 weeks, shaking the jar once a day.

After 2 weeks, strain the liquid through a cheesecloth-lined funnel into a clean quart-sized jar to remove the solids. Repeat until all of the sediment has been filtered out. Squeeze the cheesecloth over the jar to release any excess liquid and transfer the solids to a small saucepan. Cover the jar and set aside.

Cover the solids in the saucepan with the water and bring to a boil over medium-high heat. Cover the saucepan, lower the heat, and simmer for 10 minutes.

Remove the saucepan from the heat and let cool completely. Once cooled, add the contents of the saucepan (both liquid and solids) to another quart-sized Mason jar. Cover the jar and store at room temperature out of direct sunlight for 1 week, shaking the jar daily.

After 1 week, strain the jar with the liquid and solids through a cheesecloth-lined funnel into a quart-sized Mason jar. Repeat until all of the sediment has been filtered out. Discard the solids. Add this liquid to the jar containing the original bourbon solution.

Allow the mixture to stand at room temperature for 3 days. At the end of the 3 days, skim off any debris that floats to the surface and pour the mixture through a cheesecloth-lined funnel one last time to remove any solids.

Using a funnel, decant the bitters into smaller jars and label. If there's any sediment left in the bottles, or if the liquid is cloudy, give the bottle a shake before using. The bitters will last indefinitely, but for optimum flavor use within a year.

Cherry-Hazelnut Bitters

Makes about 20 ounces

---

¹/₂ cup lightly toasted and skinned hazelnuts

¹/₂ cup dried tart or sour cherries

2 tablespoons devil's club root

¹/₂ teaspoon schizandra berries

¹/₂ teaspoon wild cherry bark

¹/₂ teaspoon cinchona bark

¹/₂ teaspoon cassia chips

¹/₄ teaspoon chopped dried orange peel

3 star anise

2 cups 101-proof bourbon, or more as needed

1 cup water

2 tablespoons rich syrup (page 92)

This batch of bitters, which was inspired by my time in the Pacific Northwest, started with the purchase of a bag of Columbia River dried tart cherries that I picked up at the Chukar Cherries stall at Seattle's Pike Place Market. Any dried tart or sour cherry will work in this recipe, but if you want to keep it authentic, you can order the ones I used at www.chukar.com. From Pike Place Market I traveled to the Dandelion Botanical Company in Seattle's Ballard neighborhood, where co-owner Brian Kern unscrewed the lid of a large amber jar filled with devil's club root and encouraged me to stick my nose in for a big whiff. "Doesn't it smell like you're walking through a Washington forest on a rainy day?" Devil's club, sometimes known as Pacific ginseng, is a shrub that grows in North American forests with a cool, wet climate, and for me it instantly evokes memories of hiking the trails around Snoqualmie Falls. Rounded out with the addition of Oregon hazelnuts, this aromatic bitters takes me back to Seattle every time I add a dash or two to a drink.

Place all of the ingredients except for the bourbon, water, and rich syrup in a quart-sized Mason jar or other large glass container with a lid. Pour in the 2 cups of bourbon, adding more if necessary so that all the ingredients are covered. Seal the jar and store at room temperature out of direct sunlight for 2 weeks, shaking the jar once a day.

After 2 weeks, strain the liquid through a cheesecloth-lined funnel into a clean quart-sized jar to remove the solids. Repeat until all of the sediment has been filtered out. Squeeze the cheesecloth over the jar to release any excess liquid and transfer the solids to a small saucepan. Cover the jar and set aside.

Cover the solids in the saucepan with the water and bring to a boil over medium-high heat. Cover the saucepan, lower the heat, and simmer for 10 minutes.

Remove the saucepan from the heat and let cool completely. Once cooled, add the contents of the saucepan (both liquid and solids) to another quart-sized Mason jar. Cover the jar and store at room temperature out of direct sunlight for 1 week, shaking the jar daily.

After 1 week, strain the jar with the liquid and solids through a cheesecloth-lined funnel into a clean quart-sized Mason jar. Repeat until all of the sediment has been filtered out. Discard the solids. Add this liquid to the jar containing the original bourbon solution.

Add the rich syrup to the jar and stir to incorporate, then cover and shake to fully dissolve the syrup.

Allow the mixture to stand at room temperature for 3 days. At the end of the 3 days, skim off any debris that floats to the surface and pour the mixture through a cheesecloth-lined funnel one last time to remove any solids.

Using a funnel, decant the bitters into smaller jars and label. If there's any sediment left in the bottles, or if the liquid is cloudy, give the bottle a shake before using. The bitters will last indefinitely, but for optimum flavor use within a year.

Coffee Pecan Bitters

Makes about 20 ounces

---

¹/₂ cup lightly toasted pecans

*¹/₂ cup whole coffee beans,
lightly cracked using a
mortar and pestle or the
bottom of a heavy pan*

1 teaspoon cocoa nibs

*¹/₄ teaspoon minced dried
orange peel (page 47)*

*¹/₄ teaspoon black
peppercorns*

¹/₂ teaspoon cassia chips

¹/₂ teaspoon wild cherry bark

*2 cups high-proof bourbon, or
more as needed*

1 cup water

*2 tablespoons sorghum syrup
or molasses*

After I'd spent some time in my home bitters lab making
orange bitters and an aromatic house bitters, coffee-pecan
was the first flavored "theme" bitters I took on. I had sampled
several homemade coffee bitters, but most were too one-note
for my taste: the coffee chewed the scenery. Introducing
pecans and finishing things off with sorghum syrup was my
way of dipping into the Southern pantry, whereas the coffee
beans and cocoa nibs (I used coffee beans from Stumptown,
based in Portland, and cocoa nibs from Theo Chocolate, which
is made in Seattle) are a nod to the artisanal flavors of the
Pacific Northwest. I've since discovered that Nashville's The
Patterson House makes a coffee-pecan bitters that they use in
a bacon old-fashioned, made with bacon-infused Four Roses
bourbon and maple syrup. The Patterson House menu comes
with a warning of sorts: "This should probably be your final
drink of the evening because the smoky bacon flavor is going
to stay with for a good long while. Even so, it's awesome."

Place all of the ingredients except for the bourbon, water, and
sorghum syrup in a quart-sized Mason jar or other large glass
container with a lid. Pour in the 2 cups of bourbon, adding
more if necessary so that all the ingredients are covered. Seal
the jar and store at room temperature out of direct sunlight
for 2 weeks, shaking the jar once a day.

After 2 weeks, strain the liquid through a cheesecloth-lined
funnel into a quart-sized jar to remove the solids. Repeat
until all of the sediment has been filtered out. Squeeze the
cheesecloth over the jar to release any excess liquid and transfer
the solids to a small saucepan. Cover the jar and set aside.

Cover the solids in the saucepan with the water and bring to a boil over medium-high heat. Cover the saucepan, lower the heat, and simmer for 10 minutes.

Remove the saucepan from the heat and let cool completely. Once cooled, add the contents of the saucepan (both liquid and solids) to another quart-sized Mason jar. Cover the jar and store at room temperature out of direct sunlight for 1 week, shaking the jar daily.

After 1 week, strain the jar with the liquid and solids through a cheesecloth-lined funnel into a quart-sized Mason jar. Repeat until all of the sediment has been filtered out. Discard the solids. Add this liquid to the jar containing the original bourbon solution.

Add the sorghum syrup to the jar and stir to incorporate, then cover and shake to fully dissolve the syrup.

Allow the mixture to stand at room temperature for 3 days. At the end of the 3 days, skim off any debris that floats to the surface and pour the mixture through a cheesecloth-lined funnel one last time to remove any solids.

Using a funnel, decant the bitters into smaller jars and label. If there's any sediment left in the bottles, or if the liquid is cloudy, give the bottle a shake before using. The bitters will last indefinitely, but for optimum flavor use within a year.

Grapefruit Bitters

Makes about 20 ounces

Zest of 2 grapefruit, cut into strips with a paring knife

¹⁄₄ cup chopped dried grapefruit peel (page 47)

¹⁄₂ teaspoon gentian root

1 teaspoon coriander seeds

6 green cardamom pods, cracked

1 teaspoon dried hops

2 cups high-proof vodka, or more as needed

1 cup water

2 tablespoons honey

After orange, grapefruit has been a popular next step in the evolution of citrus bitters. This bitters offers a great way to add a kick of complex citrus flavor to clear spirits such as gin, white rum, and silver tequila.

Place all of the ingredients except for the vodka, honey, and water in a quart-sized Mason jar or other large glass container with a lid. Pour in the 2 cups of vodka, adding more if necessary so that all the ingredients are covered. Seal the jar and store at room temperature out of direct sunlight for 2 weeks, shaking the jar once a day.

After 2 weeks, strain the liquid through a cheesecloth-lined funnel into a clean quart-sized jar to remove the solids. Repeat until all of the sediment has been filtered out. Squeeze the cheesecloth over the jar to release any excess liquid and transfer the solids to a small saucepan. Cover the jar and set aside.

Cover the solids in the saucepan with the water and bring to a boil over medium-high heat. Cover the saucepan, lower the heat, and simmer for 10 minutes.

Remove the saucepan from the heat and let cool completely. Once cooled, add the contents of the saucepan (both liquid and solids) to another quart-sized Mason jar. Cover the jar and store at room temperature out of direct sunlight for 1 week, shaking the jar daily.

After 1 week, strain the jar with the liquid and solids through a cheesecloth-lined funnel into a clean quart-sized Mason jar. Repeat until all of the sediment has been filtered out. Discard the solids. Add this liquid to the jar containing the original vodka solution.

Add the honey to the jar and stir to incorporate, then cover and shake the jar to fully dissolve the honey.

Allow the mixture to stand at room temperature for 3 days. At the end of the 3 days, skim off any debris that floats to the surface and pour the mixture through a cheesecloth-lined funnel one last time to remove any solids.

Using a funnel, decant the bitters into smaller jars and label. If there's any sediment left in the bottles, or if the liquid is cloudy, give the bottle a shake before using. The bitters will last indefinitely, but for optimum flavor use within a year.

Husk Cherry Bitters

Makes about 20 ounces

1¹/₂ cups husk cherries

Zest of 1 lemon, cut into strips with a paring knife

¹/₂ teaspoon orris root

¹/₄ teaspoon gentian root

5 green cardamom pods, cracked

2 cups high-proof rye, or more as needed

1 cup water

2 tablespoons agave nectar

Husk cherries first appeared on my radar a few years ago when Seattle bartender David Nelson mentioned that he had made a tincture with them. He called them ground cherries, and this late-summer heirloom relative of the tomato travels under several names, including cape gooseberries. Ensconced in paper-thin straw-colored husks, they resemble gooseberries or tomatillos, but tear back the husk and you'll discover a blueberry-sized golden-yellow orb. Take a bite and you'll pick up flavors of honey and mango with an earthy background and sweet floral finish—the taste has been described as a cross between a strawberry and a tomato. I picked up a few pints at the New Amsterdam market in lower Manhattan and, taking a cue from Nelson, played around with making bitters. These also make a stellar flavored syrup for cocktails. Both work nicely with tequila drinks.

Remove the husk from the fruit and, using a toothpick, poke several holes into each husk cherry.

Place all of the ingredients except for the rye, water, and agave nectar in a quart-sized Mason jar or other large glass container with a lid. Pour in the 2 cups of rye, adding more if necessary so that all of the ingredients are covered. Seal the jar and store at room temperature out of direct sunlight for 2 weeks, shaking the jar once a day.

After 2 weeks, strain the liquid through a cheesecloth-lined funnel into a clean quart-sized jar to remove the solids. Repeat until all of the sediment has been filtered out. Squeeze the cheesecloth over the jar to release any excess liquid and transfer the solids to a small saucepan. Cover the jar and set aside.

Cover the solids in the saucepan with the water and bring to a boil over medium-high heat. Cover the saucepan, lower the heat, and simmer for 10 minutes.

Remove the saucepan from the heat and let cool completely. Once cooled, add the contents of the saucepan (both liquid and solids) to another quart-sized Mason jar. Cover the jar and store at room temperature out of direct sunlight for 1 week, shaking the jar daily.

After 1 week, strain the jar with the liquid and solids through a cheesecloth-lined funnel into a quart-sized Mason jar. Repeat until all of the sediment has been filtered out. Discard the solids. Add this liquid to the jar containing the original rye solution.

Add the agave nectar to the jar and stir to incorporate, then cover and shake the jar to fully dissolve.

Allow the mixture to stand at room temperature for 3 days. At the end of the 3 days, skim off any debris that floats to the surface and pour the mixture through a cheesecloth-lined funnel one last time to remove any solids.

Using a funnel, decant the bitters into smaller jars and label. If there's any sediment left in the bottles, or if the liquid is cloudy, give the bottle a shake before using. The bitters will last indefinitely, but for optimum flavor use within a year.

Key Lime Bitters

Makes about 20 ounces

---

*Zest of 4 limes, cut into strips
with a paring knife*

*2 tablespoons grated key
lime zest*

*2 tablespoons chopped dried
lime peel (page 47)*

1 teaspoon white peppercorns

¹/₂ teaspoon caraway seed

1 lemongrass stalk, chopped

¹/₂ teaspoon gentian root

1 teaspoon dried hops

*2 cups high-proof dark rum,
or more as needed*

1 cup water

*2 tablespoons rich syrup
(page 92)*

Using Gosling's Black Seal 151-proof rum brings a splash of "island spice" aromatics to this batch of citrus bitters. It's terrific with tropical drinks and rum coolers like a Dark and Stormy or Cuba libre and can bring a complex citrus note to a classic gin and tonic. Instead of cutting the zest of the key limes into strips, I recommend grating it with a Microplane. This extracts the maximum amount of lime flavor, and saves you the hassle of trying to peel the small fruits.

Place all of the ingredients except for the rum, water, and rich syrup in a quart-sized Mason jar or other large glass container with a lid. Pour in the 2 cups of rum, adding more if necessary so that all of the ingredients are covered. Seal the jar and store at room temperature out of direct sunlight for 2 weeks, shaking the jar once a day.

After 2 weeks, strain the liquid through a cheesecloth-lined funnel into a clean quart-sized jar to remove the solids. Repeat until all of the sediment has been filtered out. Squeeze the cheesecloth over the jar to release any excess liquid and transfer the solids to a small saucepan. Cover the jar and set aside.

Cover the solids in the saucepan with the water and bring to a boil over medium-high heat. Cover the saucepan, lower the heat, and simmer for 10 minutes.

Remove the saucepan from the heat and let cool completely. Once cooled, add the contents of the saucepan (both liquid and solids) to another quart-sized Mason jar. Cover the jar and store at room temperature out of direct sunlight for 1 week, shaking the jar daily.

After 1 week, strain the jar with the liquids and solids through a cheesecloth-lined funnel into a clean quart-sized Mason jar. Repeat until all of the sediment has been filtered out. Discard the solids. Add this liquid to the jar containing the original rum solution.

Add the rich syrup to the jar and stir to incorporate, then cover and shake the jar to fully dissolve.

Allow the mixture to stand at room temperature for 3 days. At the end of the 3 days, skim off any debris that floats to the surface and pour the mixture through a cheesecloth-lined funnel one last time to remove any solids.

Using a funnel, decant the bitters into smaller jars and label. If there's any sediment left in the bottles, or if the liquid is cloudy, give the bottle a shake before using. The bitters will last indefinitely, but for optimum flavor use within a year.

Maggie's Rhubarb Bitters

Makes about 20 ounces

1 1/2 cups chopped fresh rhubarb

Zest of 1/2 grapefruit, cut into strips with a paring knife

Zest of 1/2 orange, cut into strips with a paring knife

Zest of 1 lime, cut into strips with a paring knife

1/4 teaspoon coriander seeds, cracked

1 teaspoon grains of paradise, cracked

1/2 tablespoon nigella seeds

1/2 teaspoon gentian root

4 dried hibiscus flowers

1/2 teaspoon horehound

1/2 teaspoon sarsaparilla

2 cups high-proof vodka, or more as needed

1 cup water

2 tablespoons honey

If you've been to an underground or buzzed-about Seattle food event, it's likely that Maggie Savarino had her hand in it. A former food and drinks writer for *Seattle Weekly* and author of a fantastic seasonal cocktail manual, Maggie is passionate about bringing food enthusiasts together in memorable settings to share unforgettable food, which she now does at Madison Park Conservatory. When she heard I was writing a book on bitters, she grabbed my arm and said, "I must give you my recipe for rhubarb bitters." Months later I called her on it, and I present here my own adaptation of her favorite springtime bitters. Maggie adds, "I favor some of these ingredients over more commonly available spice shop ingredients because of their cool-ass names, but also for their more subtle and complex flavors." In addition to using her bitters to liven up cheap sake, she likes to combine it with rye, a splash of Dolin Vermouth de Chambéry Blanc, and two drops of orange-flower water.

Place all of the ingredients except for the vodka, water, and honey in a quart-sized Mason jar or other large glass container with a lid. Pour in the 2 cups of vodka, adding more if necessary so that all of the ingredients are covered. Seal the jar and store at room temperature out of direct sunlight for 2 weeks, shaking the jar once a day.

After 2 weeks, strain the liquid through a cheesecloth-lined funnel into a clean quart-sized jar to remove the solids. Repeat until all of the sediment has been filtered out. Squeeze the cheesecloth over the jar to release any excess liquid and transfer the solids to a small saucepan. Cover the jar and set aside.

Cover the solids in the saucepan with the water and bring to a boil over medium-high heat. Cover the saucepan, lower the heat, and simmer for 10 minutes.

Remove the saucepan from the heat and let cool completely. Once cooled, add the contents of the saucepan (both liquid and solids) to another quart-sized Mason jar. Cover the jar and store at room temperature out of direct sunlight for 1 week, shaking the jar daily.

After 1 week, strain the jar with the liquids and solids through a cheesecloth-lined funnel into a clean quart-sized Mason jar. Repeat until all of the sediment has been filtered out. Discard the solids. Add this liquid to jar containing the original vodka solution.

Add the honey to the solution and stir to incorporate, then cover and give the jar a shake to fully dissolve.

Allow the mixture to stand at room temperature for 3 days. At the end of the 3 days, skim off any debris that floats to the surface and pour the mixture through a cheesecloth-lined funnel one last time to remove any solids.

Using a funnel, decant the bitters into smaller jars and label. If there's any sediment left in the bottles, or if the liquid is cloudy, give the bottle a shake before using. The bitters will last indefinitely, but for optimum flavor use within a year.

Meyer Lemon Bitters

Makes about 20 ounces

Zest of 4 Meyer lemons, cut into strips with a paring knife

Zest of 1 lemon, cut into strips with a paring knife

2 tablespoons chopped dried lemon peel (page 47)

6 green cardamom pods, cracked

1/4 teaspoon coriander seeds

1/2 teaspoon gentian root

1/4 teaspoon dried hops

1/4 teaspoon white peppercorns

1 lemongrass stalk, chopped

2 cups high-proof vodka, or more as needed

1 cup water

2 tablespoons rich syrup (page 92)

The Bitter Truth introduced the first lemon bitters on the commercial market, and since then this flavor profile has become increasingly popular on the bitters scene. I like to use Meyer lemons, which are a bit sweeter than traditional lemons, for an unexpected flourish. Add these bitters to vodka, gin, and tequila drinks; they are terrific in a Manhattan, too.

Place all of the ingredients except for the vodka, water, and rich syrup in a quart-sized Mason jar or other large glass container with a lid. Pour in the 2 cups of vodka, adding more if necessary so that all of the ingredients are covered. Seal the jar and store at room temperature out of direct sunlight for 2 weeks, shaking the jar once a day.

After 2 weeks, strain the liquid through a cheesecloth-lined funnel into a clean quart-sized jar to remove the solids. Repeat until all of the sediment has been filtered out. Squeeze the cheesecloth over the jar to release any excess liquid and transfer the solids to a small saucepan. Cover the jar and set aside.

Cover the solids in the saucepan with the water and bring to a boil over medium-high heat. Cover the saucepan, lower the heat, and simmer for 10 minutes.

Remove the saucepan from the heat and let cool completely. Once cooled, add the contents of the saucepan (both liquid and solids) to another quart-sized Mason jar. Cover the jar and store at room temperature out of direct sunlight for 1 week, shaking the jar daily.

After 1 week, strain the jar with the liquid and solids through a cheesecloth-lined funnel into a clean quart-sized Mason jar. Repeat until all of the sediment has been filtered out. Discard the solids. Add this liquid to the jar containing the original vodka solution.

Add the rich syrup to the solution and stir to incorporate, then cover and give the jar a shake to fully dissolve.

Allow the bitters mixture to stand at room temperature for 3 days. At the end of the 3 days, skim off any debris that floats to the surface and pour the mixture through a cheesecloth-lined funnel one last time to remove any solids.

Using a funnel, decant the bitters into smaller jars and label. If there's any sediment left in the bottles, or if the liquid is cloudy, give the bottle a shake before using. The bitters will last indefinitely, but for optimum flavor use within a year.

Orange Bitters

Makes about 20 ounces

Zest of 3 oranges, cut into strips with a paring knife

¼ cup chopped dried orange peel (page 47)

4 cloves

8 green cardamom pods, cracked

¼ teaspoon coriander seeds

½ teaspoon gentian root

¼ teaspoon allspice berries

2 cups high-proof vodka, or more as needed

1 cup water

2 tablespoons rich syrup (page 92)

Next to aromatic bitters, orange bitters have the longest historical pedigree and are the most versatile. Gary Regan has been generous in sharing his recipe for version No. 5 of his orange bitters in his books and online, offering many bitters enthusiasts a jumping-off point to create their first batch of homemade bitters. With this batch I tried to achieve the spicy-citrus balance that you get when mixing equal parts Regans' Orange Bitters No. 6 and Fee Brothers West Indian Orange Bitters. The classic martini is the perfect application for these, but watch them do their magic in bourbon and rye.

Place all of the ingredients except for the vodka, water, and rich syrup in a quart-sized Mason jar or other large glass container with a lid. Pour in the 2 cups of vodka, adding more if necessary so that all the ingredients are covered. Seal the jar and store at room temperature out of direct sunlight for 2 weeks, shaking the jar once a day.

After 2 weeks, strain the liquid through a cheesecloth-lined funnel into a clean quart-sized jar to remove the solids. Repeat until all of the sediment has been filtered out. Squeeze the cheesecloth over the jar to release any excess liquid and transfer the solids to a small saucepan. Cover the jar and set aside.

Cover the solids in the saucepan with the water and bring to a boil over medium-high heat. Cover the saucepan, lower the heat, and simmer for 10 minutes.

Remove the saucepan from the heat and let cool completely. Once cooled, add the contents of the saucepan (both liquid and solids) to another quart-sized Mason jar. Cover the jar and store at room temperature out of direct sunlight for 1 week, shaking the jar daily.

After 1 week, strain the jar with the liquid and solids through a cheesecloth-lined funnel into a clean quart-sized Mason jar. Repeat until all of the sediment has been filtered out. Discard the solids. Add this liquid to jar containing the original vodka solution.

Add the rich syrup to the solution and stir to incorporate, then cover and give the jar a shake to fully dissolve.

Allow the mixture to stand at room temperature for 3 days. At the end of the 3 days, skim off any debris that floats to the surface and pour the mixture through a cheesecloth-lined funnel one last time to remove any solids.

Using a funnel, decant the bitters into smaller jars and label. If there's any sediment left in the bottles, or if the liquid is cloudy, give the bottle a shake before using. The bitters will last indefinitely, but for optimum flavor use within a year.

Pear Bitters

Makes about 20 ounces

3 Bartlett pears, cored and
coarsely chopped

Zest of 1 lemon, cut into
strips with a paring knife

1 cinnamon stick

$1/4$ teaspoon allspice berries

$1/4$ teaspoon black
peppercorns

$1/2$ teaspoon cinchona bark

$1/4$ teaspoon callamus root

4 cloves

1 vanilla bean, halved
lengthwise and seeds
scraped out (use both
pod and seeds)

3-inch knob of fresh ginger,
peeled and coarsely
chopped

2 cups high-proof vodka, or
more as needed

1 cup water

2 tablespoons rich syrup
(page 92)

My first taste of pear bitters came upon my inaugural visit to Prime Meats in Carroll Gardens, Brooklyn, where I met mixologist Damon Boelte, who, inspired by the pear tree that's visible from the restaurant's back dining room, created a house bitters to use in their old-fashioned, which is made with spicy Rittenhouse 100-proof rye. Damon also mixes up a signature Buddha's hand bitters—made with the fingered citrus fruit that resembles a bright yellow sea creature—that's used in the restaurant's house Manhattan. Damon has dropped some hints about his technique and what goes into the mix, but, like many bitters makers, he can be a little elusive. Taking advantage of fall farmers' markets, I've played around with using small, sweet Seckel pears, but Bartletts really bring the classic pear flavor to the mix.

Place all of the ingredients except for the vodka, water, and rich syrup in a quart-sized Mason jar or other large glass container with a lid. Pour in the 2 cups of vodka, adding more if necessary so that all the ingredients are covered. Seal the jar and store at room temperature out of direct sunlight for 2 weeks, shaking the jar once a day.

After 2 weeks, strain the liquid through a cheesecloth-lined funnel into a clean quart-sized jar to remove the solids. Repeat until all of the sediment has been filtered out. Squeeze the cheesecloth over the jar to release any excess liquid and transfer the solids to a small saucepan. Cover the jar and set aside.

Cover the solids in the saucepan with the water and bring to a boil over medium-high heat. Cover the saucepan, lower the heat, and simmer for 10 minutes.

Remove the saucepan from the heat and let cool completely. Once cooled, add the contents of the saucepan (both liquid and solids) to another quart-sized Mason jar. Cover the jar and store at room temperature out of direct sunlight for 1 week, shaking the jar daily.

After 1 week, strain the jar with the liquid and solids through a cheesecloth-lined funnel into a clean quart-sized Mason jar. Repeat until all of the sediment has been filtered out. Discard the solids. Add this liquid to jar containing the original vodka solution.

Add the rich syrup to the solution and stir to incorporate, then cover and give the jar a shake to fully dissolve.

Allow the mixture to stand at room temperature for 3 days. At the end of the 3 days, skim off any debris that floats to the surface and pour the mixture through a cheesecloth-lined funnel one last time to remove any solids.

Using a funnel, decant the bitters into smaller jars and label. If there's any sediment left in the bottles, or if the liquid is cloudy, give the bottle a shake before using. The bitters will last indefinitely, but for optimum flavor use within a year.

Root Beer Bitters

Makes about 20 ounces

---

*Zest of ¹/₂ orange, cut into
strips with a paring knife*

*Zest of ¹/₂ lemon, cut into
strips with a paring knife*

*¹/₂ teaspoon sassafras
(optional)*

¹/₂ teaspoon sarsaparilla

¹/₂ teaspoon licorice root

¹/₄ teaspoon dried hyssop

¹/₄ teaspoon dried wintergreen

¹/₄ teaspoon dried spearmint

¹/₂ teaspoon cassia chips

1 cinnamon stick

*2 cups high-proof bourbon, or
more as needed*

1 cup water

*2 tablespoons rich syrup
(page 92)*

The primary reason for the dearth of commercial root beer bitters is the fact that the FDA banned sassafras, whose root bark was a key ingredient in authentic root beer, as an additive in 1960. The safrole oil in sassafras was linked to liver cancer in rats, but tests were never conducted on humans, and there are conflicting views on the carcinogenic nature of sassafras. Powdered sassafras is still used in filé powder, a key ingredient for making gumbo, and home-brew enthusiasts haven't let the FDA stop them from using it either. Even if it isn't labeled as such, the sassafras you might come across at your herbalist has been stripped of the safrole oil, along with much of its original flavor. Considering that bitters are used in a concentrated dash at a time, which results in a low dosage of safole oil, I'll leave it up to you whether you want to use it or not (I do, and I'm still standing), but use a trusted herbal shop that can give you the skinny on sassafras. This is one of my favorite homemade bitters, and I just love a dash or two in a bourbon old-fashioned made with rich simple syrup and garnished with a fat orange peel.

Place all of the ingredients except for the bourbon, water, and rich syrup in a quart-sized Mason jar or other large glass container with a lid. Pour in the 2 cups of bourbon, adding more if necessary so that all the ingredients are covered. Seal the jar and store at room temperature out of direct sunlight for 2 weeks, shaking the jar once a day.

After 2 weeks, strain the liquid through a cheesecloth-lined funnel into a clean quart-sized jar to remove the solids. Repeat until all of the sediment has been filtered out. Squeeze the cheesecloth over the jar to release any excess liquid and transfer the solids to a small saucepan. Cover the jar and set aside.

Cover the solids in the saucepan with the water and bring to a boil over medium-high heat. Cover the saucepan, lower the heat, and simmer for 10 minutes.

Remove the saucepan from the heat and let cool completely. Once cooled, add the contents of the saucepan (both liquid and solids) to another quart-sized Mason jar. Cover the jar and store at room temperature out of direct sunlight for 1 week, shaking the jar daily.

After 1 week, strain the jar with the liquids and solids through a cheesecloth-lined funnel into a quart-sized Mason jar. Repeat until all of the sediment has been filtered out. Discard the solids. Add this liquid to the jar containing the original bourbon solution.

Add the rich syrup to the solution and stir to incorporate, then cover and give the jar a shake to fully dissolve.

Allow the mixture to stand at room temperature for 3 days. At the end of the 3 days, skim off any debris that floats to the surface and pour the mixture through a cheesecloth-lined funnel one last time to remove any solids.

Using a funnel, decant the bitters into smaller jars and label. If there's any sediment left in the bottles, or if the liquid is cloudy, give the bottle a shake before using. The bitters will last indefinitely, but for optimum flavor use within a year.

SETTING UP
YOUR BAR

Now that you know more about bitters, and maybe have even been inspired to make your own, let's make some drinks to put them to work. But first, here are some thoughts on the tools you'll want to have on hand.

BASIC BAR TOOLS

You don't have to own each and every implement listed below in order to make killer cocktails—the less essential tools are noted as such—but I find that all of these are useful items to have in your kit. I've picked up most of my gear at restaurant supply stores, at cookware stores, or online at Amazon.com, The Boston Shaker (www.thebostonshaker.com), or Cocktail Kingdom (www.cocktailkingdom.com).

Jigger or Measuring Cup

Shaped like an hourglass, the classic jigger is a metal measuring device made up of two conical cups, one on each side, measuring 1 ounce (pony) and 1¹/₂ ounces (jigger). Jiggers are also available in different measurements (such as 2 ounces/1 ounce and 1 ounce/¹/₂ ounce, for example), but if you're going to own only one, start with the classic. Alternatively, you can use a shot glass with measurement marks. I'm a fan of OXO's stainless-steel 2-ounce angled liquid measuring cups. The angled spout makes for a clean pour, and the measurements are easy to read from above. Resist the temptation to free-pour your spirits at home. While there's always room for improvisation when creating and mixing drinks, accurately measuring your ingredients is key to creating a well-balanced cocktail.

Boston Shaker

This shaker is the standard one used by bartenders. Using it properly can take some practice, but it's well worth the effort. The shaker consists of two parts: a heavy-bottomed, tempered 16-ounce glass (a standard pint glass will do) and a larger stainless-steel cup (the ones I use are 28 ounces). (You'll also see Boston shakers that use two tins rather than a glass-and-tin combination.) Add your ice and cocktail ingredients to the clear mixing glass (being able to see the ingredients is one of the major benefits of using the Boston shaker), and then cover the glass with the metal tin at a slight angle. Give the bottom of the metal tin a tap with the heel of your hand to create a seal. You should now be able to lift the connected shakers with one hand, but there's no need to show off. Invert the connected shakers so the glass is now on top and, using two hands, shake the ingredients until well chilled—the sides of the metal tin will begin to frost up. Set the shaker back down on your work surface, tin side down, and, with the heel of your hand, tap the tin near where it meets the glass, on the side toward which the tin is leaning, to break the seal.

Cobbler Shaker

An alternative to the Boston shaker is the cobbler shaker, which consists of three parts: a shaker, a lid with a spout and built-in strainer, and a cap for the lid. While the built-in strainer is convenient, the spouts are typically on the smaller side, and fresh ingredients like muddled herbs and fruit pulp tend to get caught up in the grill. Most cobbler shakers are made of stainless steel, but some do come with glass bases. I keep a number of vintage glass cobbler shakers that I inherited from my father out on my bar at home, but I use a Boston shaker for mixing drinks.

Mixing Glass

You can use a pint glass or the glass half of a Boston shaker to mix drinks, but, like many professional bartenders, I've grown attached to the heavy-bottomed Yarai mixing glasses from Japan. Available in a basic model or a more elegant seamless variety, these are pleasing to the eye, feel great in the hand, and have a lipped edge and spout for ease of pouring.

Hawthorn Strainer

This metal strainer is used in tandem with the Boston shaker to hold back the ice you used to mix your drink and any loose ingredients, such as herbs, fruit, or pulp. It features two to four prongs that keep the strainer from slipping into the shaker and a flexible metal coil for a snug fit. I really like the ergonomic design of OXO's cocktail strainer for its natural fit in the hand and its short handle, which doesn't get in the way like other strainer handles often do.

Julep Strainer

This metal strainer resembles a big slotted spoon with a short handle and a perforated convex base. You use this strainer with stirred drinks or when pouring from a mixing glass by placing the strainer in the glass at an angle, concave side down, keeping it secure with a finger or two where the handle

meets the glass. As long as there's a snug fit, you can get away with using a Hawthorn strainer for most of your straining needs, but if the drink contains fresh herbs (like those in a mint julep, page 135), they can get caught up in the coil. And if you're pouring a julep, a julep strainer seems to be in order, no?

Tea Strainer

This small fine-mesh strainer is used to double-strain drinks, particularly those that contain fresh fruit juices or eggs. Simply hold the tea strainer over your glass and pour your strained drink from the shaker through the tea strainer.

Bar Spoon

A metal spoon that is at least 10 inches long and has a spiral handle, a bar spoon is used for stirring drinks in a glass. It also comes in handy for layering drinks (stacking spirits of different densities—and often different colors—in a clear glass so you can see each individual layer), adding a teaspoon of syrup or sugar, hand-cracking ice, or ladling a few drops of a cocktail you're mixing on the back of your hand to taste for balance. More ornate bar spoons—some weighted with pestles on the opposite end for muddling or adorned with tridents for spearing garnishes—are increasingly popular with bartenders, but basic bar spoons are inexpensive and easy to find at restaurant supply stores.

Muddler

You could get away with using a wooden spoon to muddle a sugar cube, herbs, or fruit in a mixing glass, but a muddler is custom-made for the job. They come in various sizes, but most look like a miniature baseball bat.

The flat side is the business end of the muddler, the side you use to gently mash fruit or a bitters-soaked sugar cube, bruise fresh herbs to release their essential oils, or even to crush ice. Muddlers made out of a combination of stainless steel and silicone or out of plastic are gaining in popularity, but I prefer using the classic wooden muddler. Just be sure to avoid one that's treated with paint, lacquer, or another coating, as these materials can chip off over time and wind up in your drink. Chris Gallagher's handmade PUG! Muddlers (available at The Boston Shaker), though more expensive than most, are gorgeous, feel great in the hand, and will last you a lifetime.

Juicer

Using fresh citrus juice is essential to making top-quality cocktails. Fresh juice doesn't keep long in the refrigerator, so plan to squeeze as you go, or, if you're going to need a large quantity for a party, juice the fruit at the last minute as you prep for the event. A hinged citrus press is perfect for lemons, limes, and smaller citrus like tangerines. Place a halved piece of fruit in the cup cut side down and squeeze with all your might. For larger citrus, such as oranges and grapefruit, or when you want to juice a large quantity of citrus, an electric juicer is what you're after. I like Black & Decker's CitrusMate Plus. If you really want to go all out, a professional hand-press juicer is a wonder to watch in action, but it's heavy, expensive, and requires plenty of counter space.

Peeler

A swivel (vegetable) peeler is essential for cutting strips of zest from citrus fruits without taking too much of the bitter white pith with it. A Y-shaped peeler has a wider blade and can be used to cut away larger pieces of zest.

Channel Knife

The deep, grooved blade of a channel knife is used to peel long, thin strips of zest, which are typically used for garnish. It can take a little practice to get used to using it and learn to apply the right amount of pressure to get the results you want. Some channel knives are single-purpose tools, but others incorporate a zester as well.

Zesters

The aforementioned zester that is a part of some channel knives produces very thin strips of zest, which aren't often used in cocktails, although you might use the zester to carve a decorative design into a garnish. What you actually need is a Microplane grater to zest citrus, ginger, and hard spices such as nutmeg. There are small zesters designed especially for nutmeg, but the multitasking Microplane will do just fine.

Knives

A 3- to 4-inch paring knife is the right size for slicing and chopping ingredients and garnishes. Kuhn Rikon makes a nonstick paring knife in a rainbow of vibrant colors. The blade is super-sharp and comes with a removable plastic sheath, making it a great on-the-go knife to have on hand for picnics. You'll also want to have an 8-inch chef's knife—either classic or santoku style—for cutting larger pieces of fruit and general kitchen prep.

Cutting Board

You'll need a large kitchen cutting board for basic prep tasks, especially when working with larger fruit like pineapple or melons. Hardwood is best (be sure to regularly treat it with mineral oil), but a nonporous polyethylene board will work as well. I also like to keep a small wooden cutting board on hand for slicing lemons, limes, and oranges. When I'm entertaining, I leave this out at the cocktail station with a paring knife, peeler, and zester.

Corkscrew/Bottle Opener

In addition to a corkscrew, the compact tool known as a "waiter's friend" also includes a bottle opener and a small blade that is handy for cutting away plastic, foil, wax, or metal wrappers around bottle tops. This, and the two-sided "church key"–style bottle opener—armed with a dull end on one side for opening bottles and a sharp end on the opposite side for punching holes in metal cans—is all you really need.

Towels

When preparing drinks, cleaning your workspace as you go is just as important to the home mixologist as it is to home cooks. Keep clean cotton kitchen towels around to use for mopping up spills, wrapping ice for cracking or crushing, or covering the top of a Champagne bottle when you're popping the cork.

Ice Cube Trays and Molds

Ice is a key ingredient for making balanced cocktails. If your refrigerator has an automatic ice maker, that's fantastic. If not, make your ice as close to when you actually need it as you can: don't rely on a frostbitten tray that's been in the back of your freezer absorbing all sorts of scents. If you're entertaining, allow enough time to make multiple batches of ice and store the cubes in zip-top freezer bags. Use an ice cube tray that produces good-sized cubes of uniform size; a 1-by-1-inch cube is ideal for mixing and serving most iced drinks. Silicone ice trays, like the ones made by Tovolo, make great ice for cocktails. I use these, but it can be a bit of a production to release the ice from the trays. The twist-the-tray approach doesn't work—you have to pop them out one at a time—but the uniform, perfectly sized ice cubes are worth the extra effort. I like keeping a few of the 1-by-1-inch trays and a larger tray for 2-by-2-inch cubes that are great for drinks served "on the rock." The ice sphere, made popular by Japanese bartenders for whiskey drinks, can be achieved at home with a mold. You can pick up an inexpensive plastic sphere mold online from Muji, the Japanese clothing and home supply store. Disposable plastic or paper cups can be used as molds for large "plugs" of ice. Finally, you can also use plastic food storage containers or metal pans to create larger blocks of ice for hand-carving or for punches—just be sure not to fill the container all the way to top to avoid the ice expanding over the lid. For best results, use filtered water when making your ice.

Ice Bucket and Tongs

Keep your ice within arm's reach when you're mixing drinks and out in the open and available to your guests. Avoid handling ice with your hands as much as possible (hand-cracked ice and hand-carved ice being the exceptions). Use metal tongs or a scoop to transfer ice to mixing and serving glasses.

The Meehan Utility Bag

In 2009, PDT's Jim Meehan teamed up with the Virginia leather design company Moore & Giles to design a bespoke carryall for the contemporary bartender. Mixing equal parts modern mixology with American heritage fashion, the stylish bag is constructed of oiled leather and waxed canvas and is roomy and functional enough to transport sufficient gear and booze to act as a mobile bar. Taking a cue from chefs' knife kits, the bag also has a removable canvas-and-leather roll-up to protect your knives, stirring spoons, ice picks, zesters, bottle openers, and corkscrews. And when your bag isn't packed with Pappy Van Winkle, bitters, and Japanese mixing glasses, you can remove the padded compartments and employ it as a handsome weekend bag. (Fair warning: the Meehan Bag and roll-up kit cost north of $700. While nowhere near as stylish, a repurposed knife roll-up bag from a kitchen supply store or a pocket-lined tool bag from Home Depot will serve, and allows you to save some money for that Pappy Van Winkle.)

Ice Pick

It's not essential—and please be careful if you decide to wield one of these—but an ice pick is handy to have for chipping chunks of ice from a large block of ice.

Lewis Bag and Wooden Mallet

Fill this heavy-duty cotton canvas bag (you can use a coin bag from a bank, if you can get your hands on one) with ice and go at it with a muddler, rolling pin, or mallet to crack or crush your ice to the desired consistency. You can wrap your ice in a kitchen towel, but the Lewis bag is designed to wick away moisture, resulting in much drier ice.

Jars and Bottles

I use Mason jars not only for prep and storage but also as drinking glasses and for serving foods like ice cream and pudding. They're great for storing syrups, tinctures, small batches of infusions, and freshly squeezed juices. I like to keep a variety of wide-mouth jars in quart, pint, and half-pint sizes in the kitchen. You can find these at hardware stores, big-box retailers, and most grocery stores. Decorative glass bottles that have a pouring spout with a stopper and plastic squeeze bottles are also useful for storing and pouring syrups and juices.

Cocktail Straws

Having these on hand is vital for tasting the drinks you're making. Dip the straw into the shaker or mixing glass, cover the top opening with your finger, and lift it out the glass, taking a sample of the drink with you to taste. You can also wrap strips of citrus zest around a straw to make an attractive coil for your garnish.

Garnish Picks

A toothpick will do the trick, but there are vehicles for your garnishes that pack a bit more panache. Acrylic or reusable metal spears are fine, but I prefer bamboo knot picks for cherries and fruit spears.

examples of classic

GLASSWARE

1. Champagne Flute

2. Old-Fashioned

3. Double Old-Fashioned

4. Cocktail (Martini)

5. Coupe

6. Mason Jar

7. Highball

GLASSWARE

I barely have the space in my apartment to hold all of my bitters, let alone a varied selection of unique glassware. However, I do have stored away a couple of cases of 8-ounce rocks glasses, which can fill in for punch cups or even short glasses for drinks served up, in a pinch. If you're hosting a larger affair you can always rent glasses from a catering company, but here are a few essentials that you should have in your cupboard or out on your bar.

For most drinks, it's important to chill your glass before serving, especially with drinks served straight up. If you don't have room to store glasses in your freezer, simply fill each glass with ice and a little water while you're preparing the cocktail and then dispose of the ice water just before straining and pouring.

Old-Fashioned Glass (6 to 8 ounces)
Also known as a rocks glass, this heavy-bottomed glass is used for short drinks served over ice. I prefer to use the double old-fashioned (10 to 12 ounces), sometimes called a bucket glass, less for its capacity and more for its heft, especially with drinks served with a single large hunk of ice.

Highball Glass (8 to 12 ounces)
Shaped like a tall old-fashioned glass, the versatile highball glass is my all-purpose glass for tall drinks served over ice. The highball's cousin, the collins glass, is similar but narrower.

Cocktail Glass (3 to 6 ounces)
The classic V-shaped "martini" glass is a must for serving classic and contemporary "up" drinks. Avoid the birdbath-sized glasses and go instead for sleek, smaller models that will hold a more reasonable amount.

Coupe Glass (3 to 5 ounces)
Thanks to craft bartenders and the general interest in vintage cocktails, the coupe glass has been making a comeback. You've probably seen this stemmed glass with a shallow rounded bowl used to serve Champagne. While the more traditional stemmed champagne flute better preserves Champagne's bubbles, there's an undeniable elegance about the coupe. It's used to serve champagne or a straight-up cocktail. Keep your eye out for vintage coupes at

flea markets, estate sales, and thrift stores. The coupe is my preferred glass for serving Champagne cocktails.

Champagne Flute (7 to 10 ounces)
Purists say that the slender champagne flute, which features an elongated vessel atop a glass stem, is the best way to experience the essence of Champagne. Since I've embraced the coupe glass I've been reserving my Champagne flutes for when I'm sipping bubbly on its own, but you can use flutes for Champagne cocktails as well.

Mason Jar (16 ounces)
For casual get-togethers a wide-mouth pint jar can fill in for a water glass, and it serves as the perfect vehicle for a back-porch cooler.

Punch Bowl
If you don't own a punch bowl, you can use a large mixing bowl in a pinch. I think it adds a bit more character, however, when you serve a punch from a metal bowl, especially if it's a vintage trophy cup that you picked up at the local flea market.

MIXERS

Soda
If you have trouble finding any of these where you live, check out www.amazon.com or www.bevmo.com.

Mexican Coca-Cola • Ginger ale (Blenheim Hot, Fever-Tree, Fresh Ginger Ginger Ale by Bruce Cost, Boylan Bottling Company, Vernors) • Ginger beer (Barritt's, Reed's, Fentimans) • San Pellegrino Aranciata • San Pellegrino Chinotto Soda • San Pellegrino Limonata • San Pellegrino Sanbitter

Seltzer/Club Soda
Use individual-size bottles to maintain freshness.

Simple and Rich Syrups

Simple syrup is an essential ingredient in many cocktails. It mixes into a cocktail much more easily than a sugar cube, which I reserve for a classic Champagne Cocktail, and allows you to better control the level of sweetness. Many bartenders use a "rich" syrup, which is simply two parts sugar to one part water. This makes for a thicker, sweeter syrup, which means that you don't have to use as much.

The recipe for rich syrup below calls for raw sugar—either Demerara or turbinado—which will not only "stain" your drink with its darker hue, but also impart a subtle molasses flavor.

Throughout the book, you'll discover recipes for other flavored syrups that deliver distinctive sweetness to your drinks.

SIMPLE SYRUP

In a medium saucepan, bring the sugar and water to a simmer, stirring the mixture occasionally to dissolve the sugar. At the first crack of a boil, remove from the heat. Let cool completely, then store the syrup in a glass jar with a lid. The syrup will keep in the refrigerator for up to a month.

Makes 1 1/2 cups

1 cup sugar

1 cup water

RICH SYRUP

In a medium saucepan, bring the sugar and water to a simmer, stirring the mixture occasionally to dissolve the sugar. At the first crack of a boil, remove from the heat. Let cool completely, then store the syrup in a glass jar with a lid. The syrup will keep in the refrigerator for up to a month.

Makes 1 1/2 cups

2 cups Demerara or turbinado sugar

1 cup water

Tonic Water

Canada Dry remains a favorite, and Q Tonic Water and Fever-Tree Tonic Water are real standouts. Use individual bottles for the best results.

Fresh Fruit Juice

Keep your citrus out at room temperature prior to use and juice as needed.

Lemon • Orange • Lime • Grapefruit

SYRUPS

Agave nectar • Simple syrup (page 92) • Rich syrup (page 92) • Maple syrup • Honey • Sorghum syrup • Grenadine (Scrappy's or Small Hand Foods recommended) • Orgeat (Trader Tiki's or Small Hand Foods recommended)

FRESH HERBS

Basil • Rosemary • Mint • Shiso

GARNISHES

Amarena cherries • Brandied cherries • Luxardo Marasca cherries • Morello cherries • Cocktail olives

SPIRITS

When you're purchasing spirits, you can't expect to fully stock your bar overnight. Start by buying spirits that you like to drink and focus on making cocktails that call for those. Also, when you're known for enjoying a certain spirit, you'll find that word gets out and dinner party guests might show up with a bottle of bourbon rather than red wine. (At least that's how I rounded out my extensive bourbon collection.) Below are some of my own favorite brands to help you select a quality bottle from each category.

Gin

Anchor Junípero • Aviation • Beefeater • Bombay Sapphire • Dry Fly Small Batch • Hendrick's • Plymouth • Ransom Old Tom • Tanqueray No. Ten

Vodka

Belvedere • Grey Goose • Hangar One • Tito's

Rum

White: Banks 5 Island, 10 Cane, Wray & Nephew • *Silver*: Mount Gay Eclipse • *Gold*: Mount Gay Eclipse • *Dark*: Barbancourt 8-Year, Cruzan Black Strap, Gosling's Black Seal • *Spiced*: Sailor Jerry • *Aged*: Appleton Estate

Cachaça

Pitu

Tequila

Blanco: Avión Silver • *Reposado*: Cazadores, Herradura • *Añejo*: Herradura, Patrón • *Mezcal*: Ilegal Mezcal Joven

Bourbon

Black Maple Hill • Blanton's • Buffalo Trace • Bulleit • Elijah Craig • Four Roses • George T. Stagg • Knob Creek • Maker's Mark • Pappy Van Winkle 15-Year • Woodford Reserve

Rye

Hudson Manhattan rye • Michter's • Old Overholt • Rittenhouse 100 • Whistle Pig • Wild Turkey 101

Scotch

Blended: Cutty Sark, Famous Grouse • *Single Malt*: Glenfiddich 15, Laphroaig 15, Macallan 15

Brandy and Cognac

Christian Brothers V.S.O.P. • Clear Creek apple brandy • Clear Creek Williams pear brandy • Courvoisier V.S.O.P. • Hennessy V.S.O.P. • Laird's applejack

Vermouth and Fortified Wine

Carpano Antica Formula • Cinzano sweet vermouth • Dolin de Chambéry Blanc • Dolin de Chambéry Dry • Dolin de Chambéry Rouge • Lillet Blanc • Lillet Rouge • Martini & Rossi sweet vermouth • Noilly Prat dry vermouth • Punt e Mes

Liqueurs and Cordials

Absinthe (St. George Spirits and Marteau Absinthe de la Belle Epoque recommended) • Chartreuse (yellow and green) • Cherry Heering • Cointreau • Domaine de Canton ginger liqueur • John D. Taylor Velvet falernum • Luxardo maraschino liqueur • Pimm's No. 1 Cup • Plymouth sloe gin • St. Elizabeth Allspice Dram • St. Germain elderflower liqueur

Amari

Aperol • Averna • Campari • Cynar • Dubonnet • Fernet Branca • Gran Classico Bitter • Luxardo Bitter Liqueur • Meletti • Nonino • Ramazzotti

TECHNIQUE

Shaken or Stirred?

As a rule, spirits-only drinks are stirred in a mixing glass, while drinks containing citrus juice, eggs, or cream are shaken. Remember, though, that all rules are meant to be broken at some point. Be respectful of the ingredients you're using and do your best to present a balanced and well-made cocktail, but don't be a fundamentalist about it.

The Dry Shake

If you're making a drink that calls for eggs, egg whites, milk, or cream, it's good to start things off with a "dry shake." This means that you combine the ingredients in the shaker but leave out the ice. Shaking without the ice allows the dairy ingredients to blend together more fully and results in a richer, frothier drink. After at least 15 seconds of vigorous dry shaking, fill the shaker with ice, and continue shaking until chilled. A little more effort is required in the prep, but the results are worth it.

(continued on page 100)

Ten Essential Bitters

The only way I could keep this list to ten was by assuming—make that *insisting*—that you already have a bottle of Angostura on hand.

I'm front-loading the deck with three orange bitters. Sure, you could get by with just one type, but the expanded selection of orange bitters available on the market today is something to celebrate considering that the product was all but extinct for more than fifty years.

Regans' Orange Bitters No. 6
Spicy, with strong notes of orange peel and cardamom. Perfect with a classic martini, and can stand up to darker spirits like bourbon and scotch.

Fee Brothers West Indian Orange Bitters
The main reason I'm including this here is so that you can make a fifty-fifty blend of Fee Brothers Orange and Regans' Orange. The resulting bitters has the perfect mix of both spicy and fresh orange flavor.

Angostura Orange Bitters

The only new bitters brought out by Angostura in their 180-plus-year history, this came on the market in 2008 and tastes and smells like a freshly picked orange.

Fee Brothers Whiskey Barrel–Aged Bitters

One of the most turned-to bottles in my collection. The barrel aging introduces a new layer of woody complexity to this bitters, which comes on strong with the cinnamon pop of Red Hots candy. Each spring Fee Brothers releases an annual batch, and when it's gone, it's gone. It's double the price of their regular line of bitters but worth every penny.

Peychaud's Bitters

One of the only commercial bitters that survived Prohibition. You simply can't have a Sazerac without this New Orleans classic.

The Bitter Truth Creole Bitters

This New Orleans–style bitters isn't just a Peychaud's clone; it's a warm, spicy bitters that's rich with anise flavor.

The Bitter Truth Original Celery Bitters

This award-winning bitters possesses a complex vegetal flavor rounded out with a spicy aroma. Perfect for a Bloody Mary, but equally at home in a martini or a gimlet.

Bittermens Xocolatl Mole Bitters

The warm cinnamon-cacao spiciness of a classic Mexican mole in one concentrated drop. Fantastic with dark rum, tequila, bourbon, and rye.

Dr. Adam Elmegirab's Boker's Bitters

This reproduction of one of the most popular nineteenth-century bitters is essential for re-creating many Golden Age cocktails.

Bittercube Blackstrap Bitters

This bitters, with a rich molasses taste spiced with clove and root beer aromatics, works wonders with dark rum and bourbon.

A Word on Underberg

Food writer Peter Meehan, coauthor of the outstanding cookbooks *Momofuku* and *The Frankies Spuntino Kitchen Companion and Cooking Manual* and brother of master mixologist Jim Meehan, described drinking Underberg as "a swift punch to the cerebellum," adding, "when I put one back, I frequently and involuntarily kick my right leg."

Created by Hubert Underberg in 1846, Underberg is a German digestive bitters made of a secret stash of herbs and botanicals sourced from forty-three different countries. The closest you'll get to an official list of ingredients is water, alcohol, and "natural flavors from herbs and roots from the genus *Gentiana*," and that Underberg is brought to maturity in barrels made from Slavonian oak. I'm convinced that, at some point in this process, a few pinches of pixie dust are added to the brew, because the results of knocking back an Underberg can be truly magical.

The inky elixir within the distinctive straw-paper-shrouded 20-milliliter single-serving bottle isn't meant to be sipped or added to a cocktail, but instead is designed to be tipped back in one quick shot, either straight from the bottle or poured into an ornate drinking vessel designed specifically for this purpose. The label on the bottle pops with promising phrases like "After a good meal" and "To feel bright and alert." It's also prescribed as a stress reliever and as a tonic that "enhances the feeling of well being."

Even the product's packaging is trippy: on the box is a lush, side-of-a-van-style illustration of a wispy maiden drifting over a kryptonite-green mountain landscape. Her arms are extended as she gathers a rainbow of flowers and herbs that are drifting away from the cometlike tail of a giant botanical sphere that resembles a crumbling moon drifting out of orbit.

And whatever you do, hang on to those Underberg bottle tops, which you can mail in for any number of slightly surreal Underberg-emblazoned prizes. These include engraved drinking glasses, crystal serving goblets, a backpack, a decorative tin that's sized to fit two Underberg bottles, playing cards, a limited-edition set of plates decorated with herbs (sea-buckthorn, sage, and rose hip), and a leather gunslinger belt with a glorious Underberg buckle and enough slots to arm yourself with twenty bottles of Underberg "bullets." And if you don't think you'll be collecting enough bottle tops to cash in anytime soon, you can satisfy your Underberg itch online. Amazon and eBay both have a decent selection of Underberg and Underberg merchandise available, including collectible tins.

Pass these miniature bottles around like party favors to unsuspecting guests at your next dinner party and, trust me, the conversation will keep on going into the night. Some people will be wary of or mystified by this strange paper-shrouded bottle, not to mention the contents within. Not everyone will be an immediate convert. There will be wincing as the Underberg blindsides your guests like a runaway toboggan on a snowy Alpine pass. Then, slowly, a warm pulsing sensation washes over them as the bitter, vaguely medicinal-tasting aftertaste lingers in their mouths. An evening of overindulging suddenly doesn't seem as discomforting as it was just moments ago as Underberg performs its fairy magic on a full belly.

Depending on where you live, locating a supplier of Underberg can involve some legwork. While Underberg is 44 percent alcohol by volume, it's classified as a food product, like most cocktail bitters, so you typically won't find it at liquor stores.

In Brooklyn, Underberg is a staple at most of the gourmet provisions stores. You can typically find it up front by the register, making it the perfect impulse purchase.

Building a Drink

When a recipe calls for you to "build a drink," combine the ingredients in the glass you'll be serving it in, rather than in a separate cocktail shaker or mixing glass. Iced highballs and gin and tonics are often "built" this way. Some drinks, like the old-fashioned, could technically be built in the serving glass—but if you're using a large hunk of ice, it's more practical to stir the ingredients together in a mixing glass and then pour the drink over the ice in the serving glass.

A Final Note on Citrus Zests, Twists, and Garnishes

Many of the drink recipes that follow instruct you to "garnish with a twist." Unless otherwise noted, a simple, thin strip of zest cut from the fruit with a vegetable peeler or knife will do. Some drinks like the old-fashioned (page 107) warrant a "thick zest," which, as described, is simply a larger swatch of zest peeled from the fruit—a Y-peeler comes in handy for this. Feel free to improvise with your citrus zests, but I encourage you take cues from your serving glass. A thinner strip of curled zest seems at home peeking over a tall Champagne flute, while a thick orange zest is more appropriate for a hefty double old-fashioned glass.

Keep in mind that twists are there for more than decoration. Before serving, twist your garnish over the drink to release essential oils from the citrus peel, then rub it around the rim of the glass before placing it in, or on, the glass.

Bartender's Choice

I believe it's essential for every imbiber to have a go-to drink order at the ready when stepping up to the bar. It can vary according to the season and the setting, but it's always in your best interests—and the interests of the busy bartender—that you name your drink quickly and with confidence (better yet if you specify your brand of liquor). This especially comes in handy when the bar is three deep and you're struggling to get the bartender's attention, but it's also helpful if you're settling in for a postwork cocktail and some nibbles at a less crowded location.

That said, when you find yourself at a quality bar, the kind of place where bowls of fresh citrus are on display, syrups and the sour mix are made from scratch, and there's a lineup of bitters bottles standing at attention (hopefully with some house-made offerings in the mix), then you're in the perfect setting to take advantage of "bartender's choice." Even if you know what you normally like, even when the cocktail menu is seasonal and inventive, by putting yourself in the bartender's able hands you immediately kick off an unspoken dialogue, letting him know that you're serious about your spirits and open to discovering something new (or, often, very old). It's the liquid version of going *omakase* at a sushi bar or submitting to a chef's tasting menu at a high-end restaurant—only it's a lot cheaper and won't occupy you for hours on end.

When I first met Seattle bartender David Nelson at Spur, he was making his own bitters and tinctures and lining them up along the bar in corked glass vials that resembled a wizard's stash of potions. He also makes his own infusions, liqueurs, syrups, sodas, and ginger beer, and he joins Spur's chefs on their daily market runs to seek inspiration from the bounty of fresh produce available just a few blocks away at Pike Place Market. Nelson is a generous man. He always entertains my questions and can riff on the historical backstory of almost any cocktail you rattle off.

Ruth Reichl was in Seattle on a book tour, and I had arranged to meet up with her after her reading to grab a cocktail. Twitter was on fire with foodies wondering where Ruth would eat when she was in town, with many savvy restaurateurs tweeting her invitations to stop by. I had e-mailed Ruth a few options, and as we were stepping into a cab she said, "Let's try Spur."

David came out from behind the bar to greet us, and I introduced him to Ruth. She looked over the cocktail menu and asked about some of the combinations. "I want bourbon," she said. None of the three bourbon drinks on the menu appealed to her, though, so I suggested she follow my lead and order "bartender's choice." We got on the subject of ice, and I'm sure David overheard us touting the merits of crushed iced. Ultimately Ruth turned herself over to David, and as we split an order of pork belly sliders he went to work on our drinks.

He came back with two highball glasses, each with a mound of crushed ice rising two inches above the rim, like a cocktail snowball. He presented Ruth's drink: a bourbon swizzle. The mix of bourbon, citrus juice, simple syrup, bitters, and soda entranced her.

Later that night I noticed that Ruth had fired off her first tweet since landing in Seattle: "Wishing I were still sipping great bourbon drink at Spur." Immediately, Seattle food geeks were re-tweeting the news. The next day, Spur offered a Ruth Reichl special: half-price bourbon swizzles.

David says, "When the guest puts their trust in my hands, I will give them what I want to make them, but keeping in mind their particular tastes and what they would enjoy. This is really fun because then a cocktail is crafted for that particular person, and when it is executed well there is satisfaction on both ends . . . and a real connection is made. It shows a mutual respect for the bartender's skill and the customer's taste."

BITTERS
HALL
OF FAME

Bitters were largely written out of twentieth-century cocktail history: over time, many of the drinks that traditionally called for bitters were either reimagined without the bitters or forgotten entirely. The four classic cocktails that follow are survivors of a sort, drinks that stood the test of time and the ones you'd most likely never encounter without a dash or two of bitters, even during bitters' darker days (at least one would hope). If you ever come across one of the following drinks made without bitters, send it back.

Old-Fashioned

Because it is predated by the bittered sling, the old-fashioned may not be the "oldest" cocktail; however, it hews closest to the original definition of the word (spirits, bitters, sugar, and water). Its origin is typically traced back to the 1880s at the Pendennis Club of Louisville, Kentucky. From there it traveled to New York City, when club member Colonel James E. Pepper took it on the road and introduced it to the bar at the Waldorf-Astoria Hotel. The original recipe is a thing of austere beauty: a lump of sugar dissolved with a little water and two dashes of bitters, whiskey, a bit of ice, and a lemon peel garnish.

Since then, many modern old-fashioned recipes have adopted the "fruit salad" approach, calling for an aggressively muddled pulp of sugary orange wheel and maraschino cherry, but the original is making a comeback. For me, tasting a supersweet old-fashioned with a bit of sugary grit on the tongue does invoke a memory of old-fashioneds past (mostly stolen sips from my father's glass), but the historically accurate drink needs no more than the adornment of a lemon peel. Using simple syrup instead of a sugar cube takes the showy act of muddling out of the equation, but the syrup easily dissolves into the drink without leaving any residue.

The simplicity of the old-fashioned means that it lends itself to multiple variations. Just mix and match your bourbon or rye with different bitters, and the sugar can take the form of a flavored syrup or even maple syrup. I'm fond of putting an autumnal twist on the old-fashioned by using bourbon, cinnamon syrup, and apple bitters.

Makes 1 drink

—

2 ounces rye or bourbon

¼ ounce simple syrup (page 92)

3 dashes Angostura or other aromatic bitters

Garnish: thick piece of lemon or orange zest

Combine the rye or bourbon, simple syrup, and bitters in a mixing glass filled with ice. Stir until chilled and strain into a chilled double old-fashioned glass filled with large pieces of cracked ice or a large ice cube. Garnish with the lemon or orange zest.

Manhattan

Makes 1 drink

———

2 ounces rye or bourbon

1 ounce sweet vermouth

1 dash Angostura or other aromatic bitters

1 dash orange bitters

Garnish: amarena or marasca cherry or lemon twist

Better cocktail historians than I have presented and debunked endless accounts of how the Manhattan came to be, so I won't waste ink here rehashing those colorful stories (see Gary Regan, William Grimes, and David Wondrich for that). While bourbon has become the de facto spirit in most Manhattans, the classic spirit for this drink is rye (though I would never turn down a bourbon Manhattan). Always stir this drink, never shake it. And a Manhattan isn't a Manhattan without the bitters. Angostura is the way to go for a classic, but I personally like to split the difference and use one dash of aromatic bitters and one dash of orange. Going all orange tends to ramp up the sweetness without bringing the spice.

———

Combine the rye or bourbon, vermouth, and bitters in a mixing glass filled with ice. Stir until chilled and strain into a chilled coupe or cocktail glass. Garnish with the cherry or lemon twist.

Champagne Cocktail

Is there anything more festive than hearing the soft pop of a cork coming out of a bottle of Champagne? That's an aural cue for celebration in my book, and while Champagne is wonderful on its own, adding a sugary, bitters-soaked kiss to the equation elevates the experience tenfold. Four to six dashes of bitters should do the trick, but you really want to soak the sugar cube, which, once the Champagne is introduced, will leave a fizzy stream of bitters pushing up through the glass.

Place the sugar cube on the bottom of a Champagne flute or coupe glass. Douse the sugar cube with the bitters and fill the glass with Champagne. Garnish with the lemon twist.

Makes 1 drink

1 sugar cube

4 to 6 dashes Angostura or other aromatic bitters

Chilled Champagne

Garnish: lemon twist

Sazerac

Makes 1 drink

---

*Splash of absinthe, Herbsaint,
or Pernod*

2 ounces rye

*¼ ounce simple syrup
(page 92)*

*4 generous dashes Peychaud's
Bitters*

*Garnish: thick piece of lemon
zest*

It is often claimed that the Sazerac, New Orleans's official cocktail, was America's first cocktail; even the word "cocktail," it is argued, comes from the word *coquetier*, the name of the egg cup that Antoine Amedie Peychaud used to serve his proprietary bitters to customers of his French Quarter apothecary in the late 1830s. The Sazerac got its name in 1850 at Sewell Taylor's Sazerac Coffee House, named after the Sazerac de Forge et Fils Cognac he was importing and using for his house cocktail. But after a phylloxera epidemic in Europe wreaked havoc on France's wine grape crops, Cognac became scarce in the United States, and rye became the spirit of choice in the Sazerac.

Jim Meehan of PDT attributes his affection for the Sazerac to the drink's layers of "atmosphere": "Why do I love Sazeracs so much? I've thought about it a lot, and for me it's about experiencing a Sazerac spatially. You have a big glass. You have a glass that's rinsed with absinthe. And a cocktail—booze, sugar, bitters, and water—in the midst of that absinthe-rinsed glass. And then that lemon oil. It has a top, sides, and an overall atmosphere."

Add the absinthe, Herbsaint, or Pernod to a chilled old-fashioned glass. Roll the glass around to coat the interior of the glass and shake out any excess liquid. Combine the rye, simple syrup, and bitters in a mixing glass filled with ice. Stir until chilled and strain into the prepared glass. Rub the lemon zest around the rim of the glass and serve with the zest resting on the rim.

OLD-GUARD
COCKTAILS

What follows is a curated list of classic cocktails, from A (Abbey) to V (Vieux Carré), each featuring bitters. Some are twists on drinks that don't traditionally call for bitters but can certainly benefit from them, a Cuba libre with bitters ice cubes being a perfect example.

Abbey Cocktail

Makes 1 drink

———

1¹/₂ ounces gin

³/₄ ounce Lillet Blanc

³/₄ ounce freshly squeezed orange juice

2 dashes orange bitters

Garnish: amarena or marasca cherry

A recipe for the Abbey Cocktail kicks off both Harry Craddock's *The Savoy Cocktail Book* (1930) and Dale DeGroff's *The Craft of the Cocktail* (2002), serving as a bridge between two classic cocktail tomes written more than eighty years apart. Most versions simply marry gin and juice, but I prefer this variation, which calls for the addition of one of my favorite aperitif wines, Lillet Blanc. The bittersweet orange flavor of the Lillet really complements the freshly squeezed orange juice and orange bitters.

———

Combine all the ingredients except the garnish in a cocktail shaker filled with ice. Shake until chilled and strain into a chilled coupe or cocktail glass. Garnish with the cherry.

Alaska Cocktail

You might think that a drink called the Alaska Cocktail was first mixed up as an icy tribute to our forty-ninth state. But, like the woozy origins of so many cocktails, the true history of the Alaska Cocktail remains a mystery. *The Savoy Cocktail Book* doesn't help matters. While most of the drinks in this 1930 collection are presented without commentary, Harry Craddock offers this wry note on this drink: "So far as can be ascertained this delectable potion is NOT the staple diet of the Esquimaux. It was probably first thought of in South Carolina—hence its name." Coming in at 80 proof, yellow Chartreuse is milder than its 110-proof green cousin and brings a pleasant amber glow to the whole affair. When I take a sip I always think of the Velvet Underground's "Stephanie Says" and its hypnotizing coda: "It's such an icy feeling . . . it's so cold in Alaska."

Makes 1 drink

1¹/₂ ounces gin

³/₄ ounce yellow Chartreuse

1 dash orange bitters

Garnish: lemon twist

Combine the gin, Chartreuse, and bitters in a mixing glass filled with ice. Stir until chilled and strain into a chilled coupe or cocktail glass. Garnish with the lemon twist.

Allegheny Cocktail

Makes 1 drink

1 ounce bourbon

1 ounce dry vermouth

1/4 ounce blackberry brandy

1/4 ounce freshly squeezed
    lemon juice

2 dashes Angostura bitters

Garnish: lemon twist

I first came across the Allegheny Cocktail in *Playboy's Host & Bar Book* (1971), which, I swear, I was just reading for the recipes. On an unrelated note, Allegheny Airlines, which now flies as US Airways, was the airline where my father worked as a mechanic at the Syracuse airport. The curious combination of blackberry brandy and dry vermouth really lets the sweetness of the brandy take flight.

Combine all the ingredients except the garnish in a mixing glass filled with ice. Stir until chilled and strain into a chilled cocktail glass. Garnish with the lemon twist.

Angostura Fizz

Makes 1 drink

1 ounce Angostura bitters

1 ounce freshly squeezed lime
    juice

1/4 ounce simple syrup
    (page 92)

1/4 ounce grenadine

1/2 ounce cream

1 egg white

Seltzer water

The Angostura Fizz appears in the "Special Drinks for the Soda Fountain and Other Recipes" section of the 1908 *Dr. Siegert's Angostura Bitters* recipe booklet, but it was its inclusion in Charles H. Baker Jr.'s 1946 travelogue *The Gentleman's Companion: Volume II* that sold me on it. Baker prescribes an Angostura Fizz, known in some circles as a Trinidad Fizz, as ideal for "whenever the climate is hot and the humidity high and stomachs stage sit-down strikes and view all thought of food—present or future—with entire lack of enthusiasm."

Combine the bitters, lime juice, simple syrup, grenadine, cream, and egg white in a cocktail shaker. Dry shake (without ice) for approximately 10 seconds to fully combine the egg and cream. Add ice and continue to shake until chilled. Double-strain into a chilled coupe glass. Top off with seltzer.

ANGOSTURA FIZZ

Bijou Cocktail

Makes 1 drink

1 ounce gin

1 ounce sweet vermouth

1 ounce green Chartreuse

1 dash orange bitters

Garnish: amarena or marasca
 cherry

Made with equal parts gin, sweet vermouth, and green
Chartreuse, the classic Bijou, which was allegedly named for
the jewel-like colors of the primary ingredients, can come
across as "bombastically herbaceous," in the words of writer
Paul Clarke. A popular modification of this drink dials up the
gin by half an ounce while cutting back on the vermouth and
Chartreuse by half an ounce each, resulting in a drier cocktail.
The "Ritz version" of the Bijou from Frank Meier's *The Artistry
of Mixing Drinks* (1934) says goodbye to the Chartreuse altogether,
swapping in orange curaçao, and dry vermouth for the sweet
vermouth. I suggest you give this original version a try. As my
college writing professor used to say, you have to understand
the rules first before you can start breaking them.

Combine all the ingredients except the garnish in a mixing
glass filled with ice. Stir until chilled and strain into a chilled
coupe or cocktail glass. Garnish with the amarena or marasca
cherry.

Brandy Crusta

Invented by Joseph Santini around 1850 at the City Exchange bar in New Orleans, the brandy crusta made its first appearance in print in Jerry Thomas's 1862 *How to Mix Drinks*. Santini took the basic cocktail formula of spirit, sugar, water, and bitters and added lemon juice as well as a most decorative garnish. (Cocktail authority Ted Haigh, a.k.a. "Dr. Cocktail," author of *Vintage Spirits and Forgotten Cocktails*, points out that the sidecar and margarita are both direct descendants of the brandy crusta.) The garnish calls for the thickly sliced zest of half a lemon dispatched in one continuous swath—what Haigh calls "a skirt of fruit peel"—that's nestled inside the glass, just peeking above the sugared rim. The size of the glass—a short wine glass or goblet is ideal—is important here. Otherwise the lemon curl will slide into the glass rather than staying pressed against its sides.

Makes 1 drink

1 lemon wedge plus 1 whole lemon

Superfine sugar

2 ounces brandy

1/2 ounce orange curaçao

1/2 ounce freshly squeezed lemon juice

2 dashes Boker's Bitters or Angostura bitters

Cut a slit in a lemon wedge and run it around the rim of a small wine glass or goblet. Sprinkle the sugar on a small plate and roll the outside of the lemon-moistened rim in the sugar to create a thick crust on the outside of the glass. Chill the glass in the refrigerator until the sugar hardens into a firm crust.

Select a lemon that's roughly the same diameter as the glass you're using. Cut the lemon in half through its equator. Working with half of the lemon, slice off the tip of the uncut end, then use a paring knife to peel the lemon, taking care to keep the peel in one continuous piece, as if you were peeling an apple. Once the glass is chilled, tuck the lemon peel inside the glass, just below the rim. Save the second lemon half for another cocktail.

Combine the brandy, curaçao, lemon juice, and bitters in a cocktail shaker filled with ice. Shake until chilled and strain into the prepared glass. Add an ice cube to the glass and serve.

Corn 'n' Oil

Seattle barman Keith Waldbauer has turned me on to many
memorable cocktails, but I am particularly indebted to him
as the man who first put a Corn 'n' Oil in my hands. The
name and origin of this cocktail remain as murky as the
blackstrap rum used in the drink, but it hails from Barbados
and makes great use of falernum, a Caribbean liqueur made
from an infusion of rum and sugarcane syrup spiced with
ginger, lime, cloves, and almonds. There are plenty of recipes
online to experiment with if you're interested in making
your own falernum, which is a staple ingredient in many
tropical and tiki drinks, but John D. Taylor's Velvet falernum,
which dates back to 1890 according to some, will do the trick.
When I asked Keith about the backstory of the Corn 'n' Oil,
he said that most people come to it via the recipe on the back
of the John D. Taylor bottle, but, as with many great drinks
consumed in Seattle, all roads lead back to Murray Stenson,
who helped popularize the drink at the Zig Zag Café, where
they doctor it with an extra splash of Coca-Cola.

You can substitute another dark rum, but you'll miss out on
the sweet depth and dark molasses flavor of the Cruzan Black
Strap. Considering its own Caribbean background, Angostura
is the bitters of choice here, but swapping in Bittercube
Blackstrap Bitters would be a choice play.

Build the rum, falernum, lime juice, and bitters in an old-
fashioned glass filled with crushed ice. Stir and garnish with
the lime wedge.

Makes 1 drink

*2 ounces blackstrap rum,
preferably Cruzan Black
Strap*

*1/2 ounce John D. Taylor's
Velvet falernum*

*1/4 ounce freshly squeezed
lime juice*

*2 to 3 dashes Angostura
bitters*

Garnish: lime wedge

Cuba Libre

Makes 1 drink

---

*Several dashes Angostura
    bitters*

1 lime

2 ounces light rum

Mexican Coca-Cola

When I heard that Jonathan Miles, the former cocktail columnist for the *New York Times*, was going to be in Seattle to promote his debut novel, *Dear American Airlines*, I checked in with his publicist to see if he might be available for a quick meeting.

He was, so on an unseasonably hot Seattle evening Jonny and I met at Zeitgeist Coffee in Pioneer Square. We took a table outside and drank espressos in the hot sun, where the conversation quickly turned to cocktails and, when we noticed a bottle of Mexican Coca-Cola on the next table, the undeniably simple pleasure of the Cuba libre. After a pause, Jonny said, "What are we doing sitting here drinking coffee? There's got to be a bar nearby." With that, we grabbed our satchels and walked down the block to F.X. McRory's, a banquet-hall-sized sports bar bedecked in Seattle Mariners memorabilia, and continued our conversation over a round (or two) of Cuba libres.

The classic Cuba libre doesn't call for bitters, but I can't resist the combination of Angostura and Coca-Cola. Rather than simply adding a dash of bitters and calling it a day, I wanted to introduce the bitters into the drink via bitters-laced ice cubes, which allow the spiciness of the bitters to seep into the drink as the ice slowly melts.

To make the Angostura ice cubes, fill an ice cube tray with water, add 1 or 2 dashes of Angostura bitters to each section, and freeze.

Cut the lime in half and squeeze the juice into a double old-fashioned or highball glass. Drop one of the spent lime halves into the bottom of the glass. Fill the glass with the Angostura ice and pour in the rum. Top off with Coca-Cola. Stir and serve.

Dark and Stormy

The Dark and Stormy is like a portable air conditioner, and it's one of my signature drinks in the summer months. Gosling's Black Seal Rum has actually trademarked the name Dark and Stormy, so unless you're pouring Gosling's and Barritt's Ginger Beer (which is hard to track down outside Bermuda), you're not drinking an official version of Bermuda's national drink. I'm pretty sure Gosling's attorneys won't serve you with papers if you choose to use a dark rum other than Gosling's, though. And adding fresh lime and bitters only makes it better. One thing I will hold you to is the choice of soda: do not use ginger ale in place of a decent ginger beer, unless you have on hand a few bottles of Blenheim Hot Ginger Ale, from Hamer, South Carolina. Standard ginger ale lacks the peppery kick this drink calls for.

Makes 1 drink

1 ounce Ginger-Lime Syrup (see recipe)

2 ounces Gosling's Black Seal rum

2 dashes Angostura bitters

2 dashes Scrappy's lime bitters or homemade Key Lime Bitters (page 66)

Ginger beer

Garnish: lime wedge

Combine the ginger-lime syrup, rum, and both bitters in a highball glass filled with ice. Top off with the ginger beer. Squeeze the wedge of lime into the drink, dropping the spent wedge into the glass. Stir and serve.

GINGER-LIME SYRUP

In a medium saucepan, combine the sugar, water, ginger, and lime zest and bring to a simmer, stirring occasionally to dissolve the sugar. At the first crack of a boil, remove from the heat. Once it has cooled, pour the syrup through a strainer and store in a glass jar. The syrup will keep in the refrigerator for up to a month.

Makes 1¹/₂ cups

1 cup sugar

1 cup water

Two 3-inch knobs of ginger, peeled and sliced into coins

Zest of 2 limes

East India Cocktail

Makes 1 drink

2 ounces brandy

¹/₂ ounce orange curaçao

¹/₄ ounce Pineapple Syrup (see recipe)

¹/₄ ounce maraschino liqueur

2 dashes Boker's Bitters or Angostura bitters

Garnish: lemon twist

The first version of the East India Cocktail—and there are many—appeared in Harry Johnson's 1882 *New and Improved Bartenders' Manual* and took its name from the location where it was most likely created. One variation involves using pineapple juice instead of pineapple syrup; other recipes omit the pineapple altogether and swap in raspberry syrup. If you don't have Boker's Bitters on hand, you can use Angostura, though David Wondrich recommends Peychaud's for its "lovely, soft edge."

Combine all the ingredients except the garnish in a mixing glass filled with ice. Stir until chilled and strain into a chilled coupe or cocktail glass. Garnish with the lemon twist.

PINEAPPLE SYRUP

Makes 1¹/₂ cups

1 cup sugar

1 cup water

1 cup fresh pineapple chunks

In a medium saucepan, combine the sugar and water and bring to a simmer, stirring occasionally to dissolve the sugar. At the first crack of a boil, remove from the heat. Once it has cooled, add the pineapple chunks, cover, and allow to steep overnight in the refrigerator. Pour the syrup through a strainer and store in a glass jar. The syrup will keep in the refrigerator for up to a month.

Fourth Regiment Cocktail

This early twentieth-century cocktail comes to us by way of the inimitable Charles H. Baker Jr., as only he can set the scene in his wonderful guide to the good life, *The Gentleman's Companion: Volume II*: "Brought to Our Amazed Attention by One Commander Livesey, in Command of One of His Majesty's Dapper Little Sloops of War, out in Bombay, A.D. 1931." Baker points out this is "merely a Manhattan Cocktail . . . spiced with 1 dash each of celery, Angostura, and orange bitters," but it's one of the few vintage recipes you'll see that cites celery bitters as a key ingredient.

Combine all the ingredients except the garnish in a mixing glass filled with ice. Stir until chilled and strain into a chilled coupe or cocktail glass. Garnish with the lemon twist.

Makes 1 drink

1 ounce rye

1 ounce sweet vermouth

1 dash celery bitters

1 dash orange bitters

1 dash Angostura bitters

Garnish: lemon twist

Harvard Cocktail

While this cocktail (more rust-colored than true crimson) dates back to 1895, like its Ivy League cousins the Cornell Cocktail, the Princeton Cocktail, and the Yale Cocktail, it has gone the way of raccoon skin coats on game day. Indeed, after a luncheon at the members-only Harvard Club on West 44th Street in New York City, I asked the well-appointed barman (who was wiping down glasses like well-appointed barmen in movies always seem to be doing) if he had many calls for Harvard's namesake cocktail. His response of "Say again?" made me think that one hadn't been ordered there since 1895.

Combine all the ingredients except the garnish in a cocktail shaker filled with ice. Shake until chilled and strain into a chilled coupe or cocktail glass. Garnish with the lemon twist.

Makes 1 drink

1¹/₂ ounces Cognac

³/₄ ounces sweet vermouth

¹/₄ ounce freshly squeezed lemon juice

1 teaspoon grenadine

2 or 3 dashes Angostura bitters

Garnish: lemon twist

Horse's Neck

Called "the great *what-is-it* of the Highball tribe" by David
A. Embury in *The Fine Art of Mixing Drinks*, the Horse's Neck
started as a nonalcoholic drink in the 1890s, but the addition
of whiskey, bourbon, rye, brandy, scotch, or even gin brought
a spirited kick to this refreshing highball. The drink, per
Embury, "degenerated" into a nonalcoholic beverage once
again during Prohibition. Bourbon and ginger ale is one of
my favorite marriages of spirit and mixer, so that's what is
recommended here.

The garnish is achieved by positioning one continuous
spiral of zest from a whole lemon so that it is flapping over
the glass's edge, invoking the silhouette of a horse's mane.
Personally, the lemon corkscrew puts me in the mind of a
pig's tail, but I suppose the Pig's Tail isn't as elegant a name as
the Horse's Neck.

Carefully peel the zest from the lemon in one continuous
spiral with a channel knife. Coil the zest around a barspoon
or chopstick to encourage a bouncy spiral. Place the lemon
zest in the bottom of a chilled highball glass, hanging the
end of the coiled garnish over the side of the glass. Fill the
glass with ice. Add the bourbon and bitters and top off with
ginger ale.

Makes 1 drink

---

1 lemon

2 ounces bourbon

3 dashes Angostura bitters

Ginger ale

Japanese Cocktail

2 ounces Cognac

½ ounce orgeat

3 dashes Boker's Bitters or
Angostura bitters

Garnish: lemon twist

Of the thirteen cocktails listed in Jerry Thomas's *How to Mix Drinks*, the Japanese Cocktail is most likely the only true Jerry Thomas original. There's nothing remotely Asian in the Japanese Cocktail—no sake rinse, no powdered wasabi rim, no cherry blossom garnish. Instead, Thomas created it to mark the occasion of the first visit to the United States by a group of Japanese delegates in June 1860. Fortunately for all parties involved and generations of imbibers to come, the group was staying at the Metropolitan Hotel, just a block from Thomas's popular bar, where the delegation surely indulged in a tipple or two.

Combine the Cognac, orgeat, and bitters in a mixing glass filled with ice. Stir until well chilled and strain into a chilled coupe or cocktail glass. Garnish with the lemon twist.

Jersey Cocktail

Makes 1 drink

1 ounce applejack

¼ ounce simple syrup
(page 92)

2 dashes Angostura bitters
or Fee Brothers Whiskey
Barrel–Aged Bitters

Hard cider

Garnish: lemon twist

In his 1891 book, *Cocktail Boothby's American Bar-Tender*, William T. Boothby recommends that one "flavor" this bitters, sugar, and cider drink with applejack. What a fine idea. Applejack, an apple brandy–based spirit, was all the rage in the mid-Atlantic states during the Colonial era. America's first commercial brandy distillery, Laird & Company, set up shop in Scobeyville, New Jersey, in 1780, and they still produce their signature applejack, known in some circles as "Jersey lightning." Angostura works wonders here, but Fee Brothers Whiskey Barrel–Aged Bitters is what I would use. This is also a great opportunity to break out a bottle of homemade Apple Bitters (page 52).

Build all of the ingredients except the garnish in a double old-fashioned glass filled with cracked ice. Garnish with the lemon twist.

Martini

Makes 1 drink

1¹/₂ *ounces gin, preferably
Plymouth*

¹/₂ *ounce dry vermouth*

1 *dash orange bitters*

Garnish: lemon twist

At the height of the martini boom of the 1990s, so-called "martinis" were made with vodka instead of gin and typically served in birdbath-sized glasses (not unlike the one Vince Vaughn hoists on the poster for *Swingers*). At the same time, "-tini" became the suffix appended to any number of questionable concoctions. The first martinis, served in the late 1800s, were often made with Old Tom gin and sweet vermouth (see the Martinez, page 134), but around 1906 the marriage of gin and dry vermouth became the standard. In *The Joy of Mixology*, Gary Regan points out that around this time a kiss of orange bitters showed up in the drink. Orange bitters remained a part of the dry martini up through the 1930s, but by the 1950s the bitters had disappeared just as the quantity of vermouth trickled down from a healthy pour to a drop to just a vapor.

Combine the gin, vermouth, and bitters in a mixing glass filled with ice. Stir until chilled and strain into a chilled cocktail glass. Garnish with the lemon twist.

Martinez Cocktail

Makes 1 drink

1 ounce Old Tom gin,
   preferably Ransom Old
   Tom

2 ounces sweet vermouth,
   perferably Carpano Antica

1 teaspoon maraschino
   liqueur

2 dashes Boker's Bitters or
   Angostura bitters

Garnish: lemon twist

We know that this recipe was first captured in print in the 1887 edition of Jerry Thomas's *How to Mix Drinks*, but, as with so many great drinks, the details of its origin remain fuzzy. One popular tale has Thomas, then working at San Francisco's Occidental Hotel, serving it to a Gold Rush–era traveler on his way to Martinez, California. Regardless of the drink's true provenance, I have to agree with Gary Regan, who, in *The Joy of Mixology*, writes: "This drink, I believe, was born of the Manhattan and is the father, or perhaps grandfather, of the Dry Gin Martini." Later he adds, "Theoretically, at least, the Martinez was a variation on the Manhattan, and the Martini is, for all intents and purposes, a Martinez."

In place of the Old Tom gin, a slightly sweeter gin that was popular in the mid-1800s but dried up after Prohibition, I like to use Ransom Old Tom, which hails from Sheridan, Oregon. What makes Ransom so unique is their use of malted barley–based and corn-based spirits, which they allow to mellow in wine barrels, giving the gin its distinctive straw-colored hue.

Note the 2:1 vermouth to gin ratio. Some contemporary versions of this drink flip that ratio, or they split the difference and use equal parts. I encourage you to at least try the original version. It's sweeter than you might be used to, but never cloying, and aromatic as all hell. And it's a history lesson in a glass.

Combine all the ingredients except the garnish in a mixing glass filled with ice. Stir until chilled and strain into a chilled coupe or cocktail glass. Garnish with the lemon twist.

Mint Julep

This Derby Day classic doesn't traditionally call for bitters, but I'm happy to see that many bartenders have been sneaking them in, especially since bourbon and bitters make a handsome couple, and the bitters add another layer of aromatics to the fresh mint. And just as one puts on his favorite seersucker jacket for Derby Day, part of the Southern charm of the mint julep lies in its presentation. Although I've had juleps in plastic cups and collins glasses, a silver julep cup is what's really called for by traditionalists. The fresh mint makes the ultimate aromatic garnish, and the short straw tucked into the drink forces you to get your nose in there to fully experience it with all your senses.

Place the 2 sprigs of fresh mint in the palm of one hand and give them a smack with your other hand to wake them up. Then strip the leaves from their stems and add the mint leaves, simple syrup, and bitters to a julep cup or highball glass and gently muddle. Add the bourbon and fill the cup two-thirds of the way with crushed ice. Stir vigorously until a layer of condensation coats the julep cup. Then add more crushed ice to the cup, so that the ice rises over the top. Garnish with the 2 or 3 sprigs of fresh mint and serve with a short straw.

Makes 1 drink

2 sprigs fresh mint

$^1/_2$ ounce simple syrup (page 92)

2 dashes Angostura or other aromatic bitters

2 $^1/_2$ ounces bourbon

Garnish: 2 or 3 springs fresh mint

Negroni

Is it true that the Negroni, with its instantly recognizable vibrant red profile, was born in 1919 in Florence, Italy, when a certain Count Camillo Negroni asked the bartender at Caffè Casoni to replace the club soda in his Americano with gin? This tends to be the most popular account of the drink's origin, but no matter who was behind it (royalty or not), I like to thank that person every time I lift a Negroni to my lips.

Made of equal parts gin, Campari, and sweet vermouth, it's a simple drink that encourages substitutions (swap Aperol for Campari; use Punt e Mes for your vermouth; introduce Lillet; try different gins). Seattle chef Ethan Stowell is responsible for getting me especially hooked on these. Whenever I dropped by Tavolàta for a late-night nibble and I ran into Ethan, a Negroni would appear in my hands as if by magic. Before moving to Brooklyn, I spent my last week in Seattle eating my way through a gustatory bucket list, and a bowl of rigatoni with spicy sausage and a stiff Negroni at Tavolàta were the first items I ticked off.

This drink relies solely on the bitterness of the Campari itself, but you can add a dash of orange bitters to amp up the bitter citrus notes, which are rounded out with the flourish of a flamed orange peel garnish.

Makes 1 drink

———

1 ounce gin

1 ounce Campari

1 ounce sweet vermouth

1 dash orange bitters (optional)

Garnish: Flamed orange peel

———

Build all the ingredients except the garnish in an old-fashioned glass filled with ice. Stir.

To garnish, use a paring knife to cut a good-sized oval of zest from an orange. Hold it over the glass between your thumb and index finger. With your other hand, light a match and then place it between the orange zest and the glass. Slowly press the edges of the zest together, folding it in half, to release the citrus oils, which will ignite in little sparks over the drink.

Old Hickory Cocktail

Makes 1 drink

———

1½ ounces dry vermouth

1½ ounces sweet vermouth

1 dash orange bitters

1 dash Peychaud's Bitters

Garnish: lemon twist

In his book *Famous New Orleans Drinks & How to Mix 'Em*, Stanley Clisby Arthur says that "according to hoary but unsubstantiated tradition," the Old Hickory Cocktail was a favorite libation of General Andrew Jackson during the Battle of New Orleans. The drink reminds me of the Cin-Cin, which was first introduced to me by Seattle barman Murray "The Blur" Stenson: a simple but achingly perfect fifty-fifty combination of dry and sweet vermouth on the rocks, which of course benefits from the addition of bitters.

———

Build all the ingredients except for the garnish in a double old-fashioned glass filled with ice. Stir and garnish with the lemon twist.

Pegu Club Cocktail

Makes 1 drink

———

2 ounces London dry gin, preferably Plymouth or Bombay Sapphire

¾ ounce orange curaçao

½ ounce freshly squeezed lime juice

1 dash Angostura bitters

1 dash orange bitters

Garnish: lime twist

"The favourite cocktail of the Pegu Club, Burma, and one that has traveled, and is asked for, around the world," writes Harry Craddock in *The Savoy Cocktail Book* (1930) of the Pegu Club's namesake cocktail. Although the sun has set on the original British colonial gentlemen's club, cocktail authority Audrey Saunders named her popular Soho cocktail lounge after the storied Burma club, helping keep the Pegu Club name, and the cocktail, from becoming history.

———

Combine all the ingredients except the garnish in a cocktail shaker filled with ice. Shake until chilled and strain into a chilled cocktail glass. Garnish with the lime twist.

Pink Gin

Makes 1 drink

2 ounces gin, preferably Plymouth

4 to 6 dashes Angostura bitters

Just two ingredients: gin and bitters. Anything but demure, the Pink Gin was a favorite of the Royal Navy in the nineteenth century, as bitters worked its magic curing everything from seasickness to indigestion. You can see why warm gin and bitters didn't catch on like a cosmopolitan, but this bitters-stained cocktail makes for an elegant and potent affair. In *Vintage Cocktails and Forgotten Spirits*, Ted Haigh suggests serving this icy cold with six "goodly dashes" of bitters. I'd start with four and take it up to six if that's your game.

A traditional method of introducing the bitters to the gin is to sprinkle the Angostura into a coupe glass and twist and turn the glass around until the glass is coated. Since warm gin and bitters isn't everyone's cup of tea, I prefer to serve the Pink Gin chilled to the bone. Try it. As David Wondrich said of the Pink Gin in *Esquire*, "It's considerably smoother than one has any right to expect."

Combine the gin and bitters in a mixing glass filled with ice. Stir until chilled and strain into a chilled coupe glass.

Pisco Sour

Both Peru and Chile lay claim to the pisco sour as their country's national drink, but it was an American expatriate from Salt Lake City named Victor V. Morris who first created this adaptation of the whiskey sour at his eponymous bar in Lima, Peru, in the 1920s. The registry at the Morris Bar was filled with high praise from visitors who raved about the signature drink, which used the namesake spirit, pisco, a clear brandy made from muscat grapes brought to Peru and Chile from the Canary Islands in the 1550s by Spanish conquistadors.

Recipes flip-flop between using lemon or lime juice, so experiment to see which way you prefer (I like lime). Rather than being mixed into the drink, the bitters are applied to the frothy surface of the drink as an aromatic garnish. Amargo Chuncho bitters out of Peru are billed as the authentic mate for your pisco sour. With a rather floral taste and scent, they lack the spice of Angostura, but if you have a bottle, definitely give them a shot.

Combine all the ingredients except the garnish in a cocktail shaker and dry shake (without ice) for at least 10 seconds to fully incorporate the egg white. Add ice and continue shaking until chilled and strain into a chilled coupe or cocktail glass. Dot the top of the drink with the bitters (this is where an eyedropper to dispense your bitters comes in handy). Delicately run a toothpick or stirrer through the bitters to create a swirling pattern.

Makes 1 drink

———

2 ounces pisco

1 ounce freshly squeezed lime or lemon juice

$^1/_2$ ounce simple syrup (page 92)

1 small egg white

Garnish: 4 drops Angostura bitters

Remember the Maine

Makes 1 drink

———

Splash of absinthe

2 ounces rye

³/₄ ounce sweet vermouth, preferably Carpano Antica

¹/₄ ounce Cherry Heering

2 dashes Angostura bitters

Named for the American battleship that exploded in Havana Harbor in February 1898 and the resulting rallying cry that led up to the Spanish-American War, this cocktail is a somewhat obscure relative of the Manhattan. Bitters weren't used in the original recipe, but a dash or two of Angostura has shown up in enough versions (and it is a variation of a Manhattan, after all) that they aren't out of place here. "Treat this one with the respect it deserves, gentlemen," implores Charles H. Baker Jr. in *The Gentleman's Companion*. Aye aye.

———

Add the absinthe to a chilled coupe or cocktail glass. Roll the glass around to coat the interior of the glass and shake out any excess liquid. Combine the rye, sweet vermouth, Cherry Heering, and bitters in a mixing glass filled with ice and stir until chilled. Strain into the prepared glass.

Rob Roy

Makes 1 drink

———

2 ounces blended scotch

1 ounce sweet vermouth

2 dashes Angostura bitters

Garnish: lemon twist

In the Golden Age of American cocktails it was tradition to christen the opening of a new Broadway show by naming a drink after it. Many of these drinks burned out as quickly as the shows closed, but the Rob Roy is still a marquee star among vintage cocktails. As in many drinks, Angostura is the go-to bitters here, but *The Old Waldorf-Astoria Bar Book* recommends orange bitters, and Peychaud's plays nicely with scotch, so I encourage you to hold auditions for all three to determine which bitters gets the part.

———

Combine the scotch, vermouth, and bitters in a mixing glass filled with ice. Stir until chilled and strain into a chilled cocktail glass. Garnish with the lemon twist.

Satan's Whiskers

Add a splash of spooky cheer to your next Halloween party with one of the best-named cocktails out there: Satan's Whiskers. The cocktail made its first appearance in print in Harry Craddock's *Savoy Cocktail Book*, and, depending on how you groom your devilish drink, you can shake up two variations. If your guests order their whiskers "straight," use Grand Marnier; if they order them "curly," use orange curaçao. Another tweak would be to use a blood orange (when in season) for the juice and garnish to give this normally pumpkin-colored drink a diabolic blush.

Combine all the ingredients except the garnish in a cocktail shaker filled with ice. Shake until chilled and strain into a chilled coupe or cocktail glass. Garnish with the orange twist.

Makes 1 drink

$1/2$ ounce gin

$1/2$ ounce sweet vermouth

$1/2$ ounce dry vermouth

$1/2$ ounce freshly squeezed orange juice

$1/4$ ounce Grand Marnier or orange curaçao

3 dashes orange bitters

Garnish: orange twist

Scofflaw Cocktail

In 1923, Delcevare King, an influential member of the Anti-Saloon League, offered a $200 prize for the person who came up the perfect word to describe someone determined to be "a lawless drinker of illegally made or illegally obtained liquor." On January 15, 1924, the *Boston Herald* announced the winning word, which had been submitted by two different people: "scofflaw." But rather than shaming illicit imbibers, the word was embraced as an outlaw badge of honor, and in less than two weeks Harry's New York Bar in Paris created the Scofflaw Cocktail, a cocktail truly born out of Prohibition.

Combine all the ingredients except the garnish in a cocktail shaker filled with ice. Shake until chilled and strain into a chilled coupe or cocktail glass. Garnish with the orange twist.

Makes 1 drink

$1 1/2$ ounces rye or Canadian whiskey

1 ounce dry vermouth

$3/4$ ounce freshly squeezed lemon juice

$3/4$ ounce grenadine

1 dash orange bitters

Garnish: orange twist

Seelbach Cocktail

Makes 1 drink

---

1 ounce bourbon, preferably
  a pre-Prohibition style like
  Old Forester

¹/₂ ounce Cointreau

7 dashes Angostura bitters

7 dashes Peychaud's Bitters

*Chilled Champagne or
  sparkling wine*

Garnish: orange twist

Created in 1917 at the Louisville bar of the same name, the Seelbach Cocktail is said to have come into being when a bartender at the Old Seelbach Bar quickly reached for a patron's Manhattan glass to catch the overflow from a popped bottle of Champagne. Like so many things, the Seelbach was lost to Prohibition, but in 1995 Adam Seger, the hotel's restaurant director, discovered the original recipe and put it back on the menu.

After much passionate pleading, Gary Regan and Mardee Haidin Regan convinced Segar to let them include it in their 1997 book, *New Classic Cocktails*. Fourteen dashes of bitters—that's my kind of drink.

Combine the bourbon, Cointreau, and bitters in a mixing glass filled with ice. Stir until chilled and strain into a chilled coupe glass. Top with Champagne or sparkling wine and garnish with the orange twist.

Toronto

2 ounces Canadian whiskey
  or rye

¼ ounce Fernet Branca

¼ ounce simple syrup
  (page 92)

2 dashes Angostura or other
  aromatic bitters

Garnish: orange twist

My first experience with this old-fashioned variation with Canadian roots came when I asked a bartender for "something dark and bitter." Without pause he went to work. A few minutes later he placed the cocktail glass in front of me, filled with an inky potion offset by a bright orange peel garnish.

The bracing herbal bitterness of Fernet Branca is an acquired taste for most, but it doesn't overpower the drink, and it helps to bring out the warmth of the whiskey—making the Toronto perfect for the colder months.

Combine all the ingredients except the garnish in a mixing glass filled with ice. Stir until chilled and strain into a chilled coupe or cocktail glass. Garnish with the orange twist.

Vieux Carré

Makes 1 drink

1 ounce rye

1 ounce Cognac

1 ounce sweet vermouth

¼ ounce Bénédictine

2 dashes Peychaud's Bitters

2 dashes Angostura bitters

Garnish: thick lemon twist

According to Stanley Clisby Arthur, the Vieux Carré was invented in 1938 by New Orleans bartender Walter Bergeron as a tribute to the French Quarter (*vieux carré* is French for "old square"), "that part of New Orleans where the antique shops and the iron lace balconies give sightseers a glimpse into the romance of another day." If you think it's tough to find a decent Sazerac—even in New Orleans—then you might have your work cut out for you when seeking a Vieux Carré out in the wild. A note on the bitters: Bitter Truth Creole Bitters work equally as well as Peychaud's.

Combine all the ingredients except the garnish in a mixing glass filled with ice. Stir until chilled and strain into a chilled double old-fashioned glass over one large ice cube. Garnish with the thick lemon twist.

VIEUX CARRÉ

7

NEW-LOOK
COCKTAILS

Although the drinks in this section are presented in alphabetical order, it would please me if you considered each one a "track" in a spirituous mixtape of sorts. There are some originals as well as cover versions, in addition to drinks that are "adapted from" and "inspired by." Give the playlist a spin and then pick and choose drinks from this list according to your taste, your mood, or even the situation. And I encourage you to follow the sage advice of Nick Hornby in *High Fidelity*, advice familiar to anyone who has ever sorted through their records, tapes, CDs, or digital files to compile a heartfelt mix: overanalyze everything, from the make-it-or-break-it first song to the overall tempo of the mix. You don't kick off your Belle and Sebastian–loving girlfriend's anniversary mix with Insane Clown Posse, and you wouldn't serve her a bourbon-based Turkey Shoot if gin's her favorite spirit.

There are times when friends remark upon my particular bias toward a spirit—say bourbon or rye—but in those instances I simply offer the "mixtape defense." It's like opening a mix with "Gold Soundz" and closing with "Spit on a Stranger": sometimes a situation warrants more than just one Pavement song. And sometimes an evening was just made for more than one bourbon-based cocktail. We all have our favorite summer beach mixtape, or the one that we always end up playing on long winter evenings, and so it should be with our cocktail menus. To that end, I've tried to offer some specifically seasonal drinks, whether it's a summer cooler like the Primo Avenue Punch or a set-your-clock-back-an-hour tipple like the Autumn Sweater. If you like, you can also get creative and remix these drinks by swapping in different bitters, taking them in a whole new direction.

So sit back, hit play, and give these drinks a "listen." Hopefully you'll discover some instant hits along with some deep cuts that you'll want to play back again and again.

The 5th Avenue Cocktail

Native Seattle barman Jim Romdall created this cocktail as a tribute to the tony address of Vessel, the bar he co-owned and managed. Playing around with Dolin Vermouth de Chambéry Blanc as a starting point, he soon came up with a cocktail that highlights the vermouth's delicate flavor but also possesses the right amount of acidity from the lemon bitters and the citrus notes of the Martin Miller's gin. Vessel moved from their Fifth Avenue location in late 2010, but by the time you're reading this they will have set up shop at a new location in Seattle to continue the excellent level of service and creativity that helped garner the bar national attention.

Combine all the ingredients except the garnish in a mixing glass filled with ice and stir until chilled. Strain into a chilled cocktail glass. Garnish with the lemon twist.

Makes 1 drink

1¹/₂ ounces London dry gin, preferably Martin Miller's

¹/₂ ounce Dolin Vermouth de Chambéry Blanc

1 teaspoon yellow Chartreuse

1 dash absinthe, preferably Marteau

3 dashes Bitter Truth lemon bitters or homemade Meyer Lemon Bitters (page 70)

Garnish: lemon twist

Añejo Highball

The Añejo Highball is a true modern classic from cocktail legend Dale DeGroff, the man who helped usher in the return of the art and appreciation of a well-made cocktail. Dale created this twist on the Dark and Stormy as a celebration of the Cuban bartenders who kept the rum flowing in Havana during Prohibition (much to the benefit of vacationing Americans). In his book *The Craft of the Cocktail*, DeGroff bills curaçao, lime, and rum as the "holy trinity of the island-rum drink." Amen to that.

Build the rum, curaçao, lime juice, and bitters in a highball glass filled with ice. Top with ginger beer and stir. Garnish with the lime and orange wheels.

Makes 1 drink

1¹/₂ ounces añejo rum

¹/₂ ounce orange curaçao

¹/₄ ounce freshly squeezed lime juice

2 dashes Angostura bitters

Ginger beer

Garnish: lime wheel and orange wheel

Autumn Sweater

We could slip away
Wouldn't that be better?

The bittersweet lyrics of "Autumn Sweater," from Yo La Tengo's 1997 album, *I Can Hear the Heart Beating As One*, serve as the source material for this melancholy change-of-season shoegazer. Serve it over a large block of ice, or over an ice sphere—even better to evoke a fat harvest moon hanging in the nighttime sky.

Made in Sicily since 1868, Averna is a syrupy, bitter herbal liqueur. It isn't overpowering, though, and is a great gateway amaro if you're interested in exploring potable bitters. Amaro Nonino is another mild Italian digestif whose caramel color and warm, spicy burnt orange notes round out the full fall flavors here. Wrap yourself in an Autumn Sweater and embrace what the season has in store for you.

Combine all the ingredients except the garnish in a mixing glass filled with ice and stir until chilled. Add a large sphere of ice to a chilled double old-fashioned and strain the drink into the glass. For the garnish, use a paring knife to slice a thick strip of zest from an orange. Twist it over the drink to release the essential oils and rub along the rim of the glass. Stud the orange zest with two whole cloves and drape it over the ice sphere.

Makes 1 drink

1 ounce rye

$^1/_2$ ounce Averna

$^1/_2$ ounce Amaro Nonino

$^1/_2$ ounce maple syrup

1 dash Urban Moonshine
   maple bitters

1 dash orange bitters

Garnish: thick clove-studded
   strip of orange zest

The Bitter Handshake

Makes 1 drink

———

1 ounce Fernet Branca

1 ounce Blood Orange
Reduction (see recipe)

1 ounce Rye Whiskey Syrup
(see recipe)

Garnish: thick spiral of
orange zest

The Bitter Handshake was the very first drink Andrew Bohrer ever served me. He had been making a name for himself around Seattle as an inventive bartender, and he lived up to his reputation when I met him at Mistral Kitchen, where he used to hold court, and gave me a drink that I still think about often.

While Andrew was experimenting with a Fernet Branca–based cocktail, one of the sous chefs presented him with some reduced blood orange juice to play around with behind the bar. From this, Andrew developed an after-dinner Fernet old-fashioned digestif of sorts, with an ingenious rye whiskey syrup subbing in for the standard simple syrup and the rich blood orange reduction serving as an improvement over the muddled oranges from poorly made and overly sweet old-fashioneds. Andrew is fanatical about his ice and he serves this over a hand-carved ice sphere. If you don't feel like hand carving your own ice sphere and don't have the right mold, you can swap in a large hunk of ice or a large ice cube. The orange zest wrapped around the ice won't look as elegant, but the drink will still be delicious.

———

Combine all the ingredients except the garnish in a mixing glass filled with ice and stir until chilled. Strain into a double old-fashioned glass filled with an ice sphere. Place the orange zest atop the ice sphere.

BLOOD ORANGE REDUCTION

This is best made using fresh blood oranges, but if they're out of season you can use freshly squeezed orange juice instead, adding some pomegranate juice and a splash of grenadine to taste.

In a small saucepan, bring the blood orange juice to a boil over medium-high heat and boil until reduced by a third. Remove from the heat and let cool.

Makes about ²/₃ cup

1 cup freshly squeezed blood orange juice

RYE WHISKEY SYRUP

In a medium saucepan, bring the sugar and rye to a simmer, stirring occasionally to dissolve the sugar. At the first crack of a boil, remove from the heat. Let cool completely, then store the syrup in a glass jar. Due to the alcohol, the syrup will keep in the refrigerator for several months.

Makes 1 cup

1 cup sugar

1 cup rye

Black Feather

Makes 1 drink

2 ounces brandy

1 ounce dry vermouth

$^1/_2$ ounce Cointreau

1 dash Angostura bitters

Garnish: lemon twist

Aside from being one of the best bitters resources out there, Seattle cocktail savant Robert Hess was also kind enough to share two of his original cocktail creations (the Trident appears on page 190). Hess makes a point of using all French ingredients (save for the bitters) in this drink, and employs a full ounce of dry vermouth, which according to Hess plays "middleman" to the brandy and Cointreau. The addition of the bitters makes it a proper cocktail, in the true sense of the word (spirit, sugar, water, bitters). Hess's original version called for his own homemade Hess' House Bitters (you can find the recipe online), but Angostura, Fee Brothers Old Fashion Aromatic, or The Bitter Truth's Aromatic will perform with equal aplomb.

Combine all the ingredients except the garnish in a mixing glass filled with ice and stir until chilled. Strain into a chilled cocktail glass. Garnish with the lemon twist.

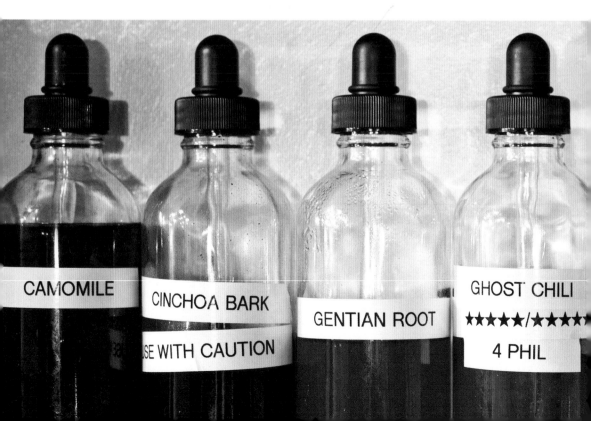

CAMOMILE

CINCHOA BARK

SE WITH CAUTION

GENTIAN ROOT

GHOST CHILI

★★★★★/★★★★★

4 PHIL

Black Scottish Cyclops

Sometimes coming up with a name for an original cocktail is a challenge, and other times it just comes to you when you're watching a YouTube clip from the multiplayer game Team Fortress 2 and you encounter the character Tavish "The Demoman" Degroot, who calls himself "a black Scottish cyclops." That's what happened to my bartending friend Rocky Yeh. Amused, Rocky thought that this character deserved a drink. Rocky describes the Black Scottish Cyclops thus: "The Ramazzotti and bitters add contrasting notes to the peat and roundness without really making it any less of an in-your-face sort of thing, like the character that it's named for."

Combine all the ingredients in a mixing glass filled with ice and stir until chilled. Strain into an old-fashioned glass filled with two ice cubes.

Makes 1 drink

2 ounces Laphroaig scotch

1 ounce Ramazzotti

4 dashes Fee Brothers Whiskey Barrel–Aged Bitters

ORRIS ROOT

PINK PEPPERC

SAS PRILLA

WORMWOOD

USE WITH CAUT

Coxsackie Smash

Makes 1 drink

---

1 lime wedge

3 sprigs fresh mint

4 sour cherries

¾ ounce Sour Cherry Syrup (see recipe)

2 ounces bourbon

2 dashes Angostura bitters or Fee Brothers Whiskey Barrel–Aged Bitters

Blenheim Hot Ginger Ale

Garnish: fresh mint sprig and sour cherry

My friends Matt Lee and Ted Lee, the award-winning food writers behind *The Lee Bros. Southern Cookbook*, split their time between New York City and Charleston, South Carolina, but they also share a country house in upstate New York, in the Hudson Valley town of Coxsackie. Depending on who you ask, Coxsackie means either "hoot of the owl" or "honk of the goose." (My money's on the goose.)

One July afternoon I joined Matt and his wife Gia on a sour cherry–picking expedition in the nearby town of Hudson. We returned home with three ten-pound sacks of cherries, and as they were being run through the conveyor belt on the farm's antique cherry pitter, I tried to calculate how much this haul would've cost us back at the Union Square Greenmarket. That weekend sour cherries showed up in clafouti, pancakes, pies, and, of course, cocktails.

If you aren't lucky enough to come across a summertime stash of fresh sour cherries to make homemade sour cherry syrup, I'll look the other way if you want to swap in some sour cherries from a jar or even use Amarena or Luxardo cherry syrup. If you're especially lucky, though, you'll have fresh cherries *and* a six-pack of South Carolina's famous Blenheim ginger ale on hand, preferably the "hot" variety. This can be hard to come by, but a spicy ginger beer will do in a pinch. While any tall glass will do, I think a wide-mouth pint Mason jar is called for here, or a glass firehouse mug from the flea market.

Combine the lime wedge, mint sprigs, sour cherries, and sour cherry syrup in a cocktail shaker and muddle until you have an aromatic, syrupy mash. Add the bourbon and bitters, fill with ice, and shake until chilled. Double-strain into a chilled Mason jar filled with ice. Top off with ginger ale. Garnish with the fresh mint sprig and sour cherry.

SOUR CHERRY SYRUP

In a medium saucepan, bring the sugar, water, sour cherries, and any of their juices to a simmer, stirring occasionally to dissolve the sugar and pressing the cherries with the back of a wooden spoon to help break them down. At the first crack of a boil, remove from the heat. Once cooled, pour the syrup through a strainer, discard the cherries, and store in a glass jar. The syrup will keep in the refrigerator for up to a month.

Makes 1¹/₂ cups

1 cup sugar

1 cup water

1 cup pitted sour cherries

Cranberry Crush

Makes 1 drink

———

12 cranberries

*Two 1-inch pieces candied
ginger, chopped*

*¹/₂ ounce Cranberry Syrup
(see recipe)*

1 dash cranberry bitters

1 dash orange bitters

1¹/₂ ounces gin

³/₄ ounce Ramazzotti

*¹/₂ ounce freshly squeezed
lime juice*

Q Tonic Water

Garnish: lime twist

Although grocers give cranberries the star treatment only
during the countdown to Thanksgiving, it's worth keeping
a bag in your freezer all year round, as their tart bite works
especially well as a flavoring agent for cocktails. The Italian
amaro Ramazzotti contains a blend of thirty-three herbs and
possesses subtle orange notes that come alive with the
additional dash of orange bitters and the warm spice from
the candied ginger.

———

Combine the cranberries, candied ginger, cranberry syrup, and
both bitters in a mixing glass and muddle until the cranberries
have popped and released their juice. Add the gin, Ramazzotti,
and lime juice and shake until chilled. Double-strain into a
chilled cocktail glass. Add a splash of tonic water and garnish
with the twist of lime.

CRANBERRY SYRUP

Makes 1¹/₂ cups

———

1 cup sugar

1 cup water

1 cup cranberries

1 cinnamon stick

In a medium saucepan, bring the sugar, water, cranberries,
and cinnamon stick to a simmer, stirring occasionally to
dissolve the sugar and pressing the cranberries with the back
of a wooden spoon to help break them down. At the first
crack of a boil, remove from the heat. Once cooled, pour the
syrup through a strainer, discard the solids, and store in a glass
jar. The syrup will keep in the refrigerator for up to a month.

Cricket Ball

I came across this understated aperitif at the Red Cat in the Chelsea neighborhood of Manhattan. So named because the drink's hue matches the color of a traditional cricket ball, the drink also matches the red décor of Jimmy Bradley's popular restaurant. What first attracted me to this drink were the bitters, of course, but also the use of Lillet Rouge, the too-often-overlooked sister spirit of the more popular Lillet Blanc. The version at the Red Cat calls for Angostura, but I've swapped in candy-colored Peychaud's Bitters to continue the red theme and Fee Brothers Rhubarb Bitters for an unexpected sour note that cuts through the prosecco bubbles.

Drop the sugar cube into the bottom of a Champagne flute and douse with both of the bitters. Add the Lillet Rouge, top off with prosecco, and stir. Garnish with the lemon twist.

Makes 1 drink

1 sugar cube

3 dashes Peychaud's Bitters

3 dashes Fee Brothers rhubarb bitters or homemade Rhubarb Bitters (page 68)

1 ounce Lillet Rouge

Chilled prosecco

Garnish: lemon twist

Do You Believe In Miracles?

Makes 1 drink

---

1 1/2 ounces vodka, preferably P3 Placid or 46 Peaks

3/4 ounce Clear Creek Douglas fir eau de vie

1/4 ounce Honey Syrup (page 166)

1/4 ounce Rosemary Syrup (page 166)

2 dashes Scrappy's lavender bitters

2 drops or 4 spritzes Rosemary Tincture (page 166)

Garnish: rosemary sprig

Mike "Twig" McGlynn and Ann Stillman O'Leary founded Lake Placid Spirits, a craft distillery tucked away in the Adirondack Mountains, where their small-batch vodkas are blended in a 220-gallon copper-column pot still using water drawn directly from the distillery's eponymous lake.

When I was thinking of ways to play around with their grain-based vodka, I immediately thought of snow-covered pine trees and raising a glass to the "Miracle on Ice," one of the most unforgettable upsets in sports history. On February 22, 1980, in Lake Placid, New York, the United States Olympic hockey team, comprised of amateur and collegiate athletes, stunned the world with an upset win in the semifinals over the Soviet team. As the clock ticked down, sportscaster Al Michaels called the action on the ice: "Eleven seconds, you've got ten seconds, the countdown going on right now! Morrow up to Silk. Five seconds left in the game. Do you believe in miracles? Yes!"

At the time of writing, Lake Placid Spirits' products are available only in New York state, so put another vodka in the game if you can't locate a bottle. But in the spirit of things, leave the Russian vodka on the shelf and use a domestic vodka, like Harvest Spirits' Core Vodka or Tuthilltown's Heart of the Hudson Vodka, both made in New York and available for purchase online. You'll need to factor in some time to infuse the rosemary tincture, but once it's ready you'll have enough to fuel an entire starting lineup with this icy, piney, wonderfully aromatic cocktail.

Combine the vodka, Douglas fir eau de vie, honey and rosemary syrups, and bitters in a cocktail shaker filled with ice. Shake until chilled. Strain into a chilled cocktail glass. Using an eyedropper or atomizer, place 2 drops or 4 spritzes of the rosemary tincture on the surface of the drink and garnish with the rosemary sprig.

HONEY SYRUP

Makes 1 1/2 cups

———

1 cup honey

1 cup hot water

Combine the honey and hot water in a bowl and whisk to dissolve. Once cooled completely, pour the syrup into a glass jar. The syrup will keep in the refrigerator for up to a month.

ROSEMARY SYRUP

Makes 1 1/2 cups

———

1 cup sugar

1 cup water

1/2 cup finely chopped fresh rosemary

In a medium saucepan, bring the sugar, water, and rosemary to a simmer, stirring occasionally to dissolve the sugar. At the first crack of a boil, remove from the heat. Once cooled completely, pour the syrup through a strainer, discard the rosemary, and store in a glass jar. The syrup will keep in the refrigerator for up to a month.

ROSEMARY TINCTURE

Makes 1 cup

———

1/2 cup fresh rosemary needles

1 cup high-proof (80 to 100 proof) vodka or Everclear

Crush the rosemary needles using a mortar and pestle and transfer to a glass jar. Cover the needles with the vodka, cover the jar, shake, and store in a cool, dark place. The alcohol will begin to turn green as it leaches the oils from the rosemary. Shake and taste the infusion daily until it reaches the desired intensity, anywhere from a few days to up to 2 weeks. When the tincture is ready, strain the solution through cheesecloth and, using a funnel, pour into small eyedropper bottles or an atomizer.

Exile In Ryeville

My friend Alex Carr and his younger sister Caroline hail
from the great state of Wisconsin, but there was something
about the Emerald City that drew them both to Seattle, where
they now work at the same company and live in adjoining
apartment buildings with views of the Space Needle. One of
their colleagues calls this arrangement a "two-Carr family."

This twist on a sidecar is a nod to Alex and Caroline's
surname and to their penchant for brown spirits; Caroline's
a bourbon and rye girl (she introduced me to the Pickleback,
a shot of Jameson with a chaser of pickle juice, a specialty of
Manhattan's Whiskey Tavern), while Alex leans toward single-
malt scotches. In fact, nearly all the single malts perched on
my shelf were gifts from Alex.

If you have trouble tracking down the small-batch bitters
suggested here, you can use Regans' Orange Bitters No. 6, but
you'll miss out on the additional smoky aromatic action.

Cut a slit in the lemon wedge and run it around the rim of a
cocktail glass. Sprinkle the sugar on a small plate and roll the
outside of the lemon-moistened rim in it to create a crust on
the outside of the glass. Chill the glass in the freezer. Once
the glass is chilled, add a splash of scotch to the glass and
swirl around to fully coat the inside, then pour off any excess.
Combine the rye, Cointreau, lemon juice, honey syrup, and
bitters in a cocktail shaker filled with ice and shake vigorously
until chilled. Strain into the prepared cocktail glass and
garnish with the lemon zest.

Makes 1 drink

1 lemon wedge

Demerara or turbinado sugar

*Scotch, preferably a smoky
    Islay-style whisky, such as
    Laphroaig*

1½ ounces rye

½ ounce Cointreau

*¼ ounce freshly squeezed
    lemon juice*

*½ ounce honey syrup
    (page 166)*

*2 dashes Snake Oil tobacco
    bitters or A.B. Smeby
    Bittering Co. Highland
    Heather Bitters or Regans'
    Orange Bitters No. 6*

*Garnish: thick piece of lemon
    zest*

Fernet and Coke

Makes 1 drink

2 ounces Mexican Coca-Cola
  Reduction (see recipe)

1¹/₂ ounces Fernet Branca

¹/₄ ounce freshly squeezed
  lemon juice

2 dashes Angostura bitters

Seltzer

Garnish: thick piece of
  lemon zest

The bracingly bitter amaro Fernet Branca has become a favorite on the mixology circuit, used either used as a component in a cocktail or on its own (a shot of Fernet presented to a fellow barman is known as a "bartender's handshake"). Fernet's North American buzz started in San Francisco, but it's also a best seller in Argentina, where Fernet and Coke is the country's most popular drink. You can certainly use classic Coca-Cola in a pinch, but Mexican Coca-Cola, which is made with pure cane sugar instead of high-fructose corn syrup, is becoming easier to find—Costco even carries it by the case now. Unlike Fernet's marketing team, which champions Fernet as the cure for all sorts of ailments (read: hangovers), I can't promise that the drink below will restore your constitution, but it just might give you a second wind and the inspiration to hit one more bar before the night is over.

Combine the Coca-Cola reduction, Fernet Branca, lemon juice, and bitters in a mixing glass filled with ice. Stir until chilled. Strain into a chilled, ice-filled double old-fashioned glass and top off with seltzer. Garnish with the lemon zest.

MEXICAN COCA-COLA REDUCTION

Makes about 6 ounces

12-ounce bottle Mexican
  Coca-Cola

In a small saucepan, bring the Coca-Cola to boil over medium-high heat and boil until reduced by half. Remove from the heat and let cool. The reduction will keep in the refrigerator for up to a week.

Gargoyle & Spire

I live in the Clinton Hill neighborhood of Brooklyn, in a building that had been, until the mid-1980s, home to the Brooklyn Cathedral Preparatory Seminary. In a nod to the building's neo-Gothic architecture, Cathedral Prep's yearbook was called *Gargoyle*, and its newspaper the *Spire*. And there's a squadron of very impressive gargoyles perched around the upper perimeter of the building. These aren't squat grotesqueries lurking in the shadows, but lean creatures with wings folded back and mouths agape, stretching out from the building as if they're about to strafe the pedestrians on the sidewalk below.

Using Strega, whose name means "witch," in the Gargoyle & Spire seems fitting. Aged in ash barrels, it's a spellbinding Italian liqueur dating back to 1860 that's made up of dozens of herbs and spices, including saffron, which is the secret to Strega's distinctive yellow hue.

Combine the gin, Strega, simple syrup, and bitters in mixing glass filled with ice and stir until chilled. Strain into a highball glass filled with ice and top off with the Champagne or sparkling wine. Garnish with the orange twist.

Makes 1 drink

---

1 ounce gin

³/₄ ounce Strega

¹/₄ ounce simple syrup (page 92)

2 dashes orange bitters

Chilled Champagne or sparkling wine

Garnish: orange twist

The Long Hello

Makes 1 drink

---

³/₄ ounce Clear Creek apple brandy

³/₄ ounce St. Germain elderflower liqueur

1 dash Fee Brothers Whiskey Barrel–Aged Bitters or Fee Brothers Old Fashion Aromatic Bitters

Chilled Champagne or sparkling wine

Garnish: freshly grated nutmeg

Damon Boelte, the bar director at Brooklyn's Prime Meats in Carroll Gardens, has an affinity for naming his original drinks after songs, albums, and musicians. His autumnal Champagne cocktail, The Long Hello, takes its name from an obscure prog rock album from the mid-1970s. (What, you don't remember the record's eight-minute instrumental track "I've Lost My Cat"?) Damon originally created the cocktail for *New York* magazine's winter wedding issue, where he described it as the perfect drink with which to toast newlyweds. This is easily one of my favorite seasonal celebratory cocktails, simple to make, elegant, and delicious. The pear notes from the St. Germain play well with the apple brandy, and the bitters and grated nutmeg add a hint of Christmas spice, making this a warm, charming, and oh-so-sippable Champagne cocktail.

Combine the apple brandy, elderflower liqueur, and bitters in a mixing glass filled with ice and stir until chilled. Strain into a chilled coupe glass or Champagne flute and top off with Champagne. Garnish with grated nutmeg.

Michelada

Makes 1 drink

Lime wedge

1 teaspoon kosher salt

¼ teaspoon chili powder

Juice of 1 lime

2 dashes hot sauce (Tabasco in a pinch, but preferably a Mexican hot sauce such as Cholula)

1 dash Maggi sauce

2 dashes Worcestershire sauce

2 dashes mole bitters

Splash of tomato juice

One 12-ounce bottle of beer, preferably Mexican beer or Shiner Bock

Garnish: lime shell and freshly ground black pepper

A basic michelada can be as simple as a beer over ice with lime and salt, but from there you can doctor your drink with tomato juice, Clamato, hot sauce, savory sauces, chiles, and more.

Traditionally, a Mexican beer like Corona, Pacifico, or Modelo Especial is used, but you can alter your michelada by using a darker beer, like Negra Modelo. The Hotel San Jose in Austin, Texas—which is the kind of place I could envision myself moving into for an extended period of time, either to finish a novel or to have a full-on breakdown—goes the Tex-Mex route, serving their michelada with Shiner Bock, a local beer from the Spoetzl Brewery in Shiner, Texas.

Bitters aren't traditionally used in a michelada, but when you're working with dashes of hot sauce, Maggi sauce (a savory soy sauce–like seasoning with a very distinctive taste, often found in the ethnic foods aisle of the grocery store), and Worcestershire, I believe there's room for bitters. Any mole bitters makes the cut here, but if you can get your hands on some of the spicier bitters from New Mexico's The Bitter End, try their Memphis Barbeque or Mexican Mole in this drink.

Cut a slit in the lime wedge and rub it around the rim of a tall beer glass. Mix the salt and chili powder together on a small plate. Dip the glass into the chili powder–salt mixture to coat the rim of the glass. Fill the glass with ice and add the lime juice, hot sauce, Maggi sauce, Worcestershire sauce, bitters, and tomato juice. Top off the glass with beer. Garnish with one of the spent lime halves and a grinding of pepper. Serve the remaining beer alongside the cocktail.

Mrs. Kitzel

Makes 1 drink

———

2 ounces spiced rum

1 ounce Amaro Nonino

1 teaspoon brown sugar

1 thick strip of lemon zest

1 thick strip of orange zest

3 dashes Urban Moonshine
    maple bitters or homemade
    Apple Bitters (page 52)

Hot apple cider

1 tablespoon unsalted butter

*Garnish: cinnamon stick and
    freshly grated nutmeg*

As a young fellow, I spent most Friday nights with my grandmother (who lived in the attic apartment above us), eating dinner, nibbling on cookies, and watching TV. My grandmother was a devout churchgoer, which explains why, during *The Dukes of Hazzard*, whenever Daisy Duke popped onto the screen in her namesake denim cutoffs, my grandmother would cock an eyebrow and whistle, followed by, "Woo hoo hoo, Mrs. Kitzel!" This was her trademark way of expressing disapproval, and one hour of *The Dukes of Hazzard* (not to mention *Fantasy Island*) provoked a lot of whistling from her.

As a child I never questioned who this Mrs. Kitzel might be, but it turns out it was a reference to *Jack Benny* regular Artie Auerbach, who played a character named Mr. Kitzel. Mr. Kitzel was a hot dog vendor, remembered best for his line "Pickle in the middle and the mustard on top!" and for his domineering, never-seen wife, Mrs. Kitzel.

Beyond a sip of communion wine, my grandmother was mostly a teetotaler, but on Christmas Eve, when my father uncapped a jug of Bailey's Irish Cream, she could be counted on to have a nip. It usually took just one sip to get her a little giddy. In that spirit, I present the Mrs. Kitzel, a hot-buttered rum of sorts, something that my grandmother might mistake for a warm cider or tea until the spiced rum kicked in and a hoot of "woo hoo, Mrs. Kitzel!" might come forth. I think it's a fine drink to have on hand while exchanging presents under the tree, or to sneak into a Thermos for a walk around the neighborhood to take in the Christmas lights on a crisp winter night.

———

Combine the rum, Amaro Nonino, brown sugar, lemon and orange peels, and bitters in a mug. Fill the mug with the hot apple cider. Add the butter and stir until it has melted into the drink. Garnish with the cinnamon stick and freshly grated nutmeg.

Pith Helmet

In an article entitled "The New Antiquarians," the *New York Times* profiled the stylish sisters Hollister and Porter Hovey, whose windowless loft in the Williamsburg neighborhood of Brooklyn is packed to the ceiling with a curated collection of mounted animal trophies, vintage tennis rackets, steamer trunks, apothecary ephemera, fencing gear, and eccentric headgear, including several pith helmets. They even have their own crest. If Little Edie and Richie Tenenbaum set up house together, it might look like the Hoveys'. Based on photos on Hollister's popular blog, I was pleased to see that the Hoveys also like to keep a few bottles of bitters on hand.

This twist on a Pimm's Cup amps up the gin-based Pimm's No. 1 Cup with an additional slug of British dry gin (Bombay will work, but the Hoveys might call for Old Raj). The lemon-basil syrup, cucumber, and black pepper present an earthy, vegetal undertone against the lemon juice and crisp bitter lemon tonic, and the bitters help bring it all together.

Lightly crack the peppercorns using a mortar and pestle and transfer to a shaker along with the lemon-basil syrup and cucumber slices. Muddle the ingredients until the cucumbers have become one with the syrup.

Fill the shaker halfway with ice, then add the gin, Pimm's, lemon juice, and both bitters. Shake until chilled and strain into an ice-filled highball glass and top with the Fever-Tree Bitter Lemon. Garnish with a basil leaf and a cucumber slice and dust with a grind of pepper.

Makes 1 drink

—

6 black peppercorns

$^1/_2$ ounce Lemon-Basil Syrup (page 176)

3 cucumber slices

1 ounce London dry gin

1 ounce Pimm's No. 1 Cup

$^1/_2$ ounce freshly squeezed lemon juice

2 dashes Angostura bitters

2 dashes celery bitters

Fever-Tree Bitter Lemon or high-quality tonic water

Garnish: basil leaf, cucumber slice, and freshly ground black pepper

PITH HELMET

LEMON-BASIL SYRUP

Makes 1¹/₂ cups

1 cup sugar

1 cup water

12 basil leaves

Zest of 2 lemons

Rinse the basil leaves in water and let dry on a towel. In a medium saucepan, bring the sugar, water, basil, and lemon zest to a simmer, stirring occasionally to dissolve the sugar and pressing the basil against the pan with the back of a wooden spoon. At the first crack of a boil, remove from the heat. Once cooled, pour the syrup through a strainer, discard the basil, and store in a glass jar. The syrup will keep in the refrigerator for up to a month.

Primo Avenue Punch

There are few places I'd rather be on the Fourth of July than sitting poolside at my sister Vicki's place on Primo Avenue in Sherrill, New York, with a plastic tumbler of punch in hand. Vicki and her husband, Bob, are fans of blueberry vodka, but, as the opinionated (read: annoying) younger brother, I'm always full of constructive criticism, which is why I swap in cachaça, the popular Brazilian spirit made from fermented sugarcane. Cachaça brings an unexpected twist to the drink, and the use of fresh fruit, both muddled and as a garnish, takes full advantage of the abundance of summer berries at the roadside fruit stands. I think Bob and Vicki would approve.

In a cocktail shaker, add the blueberries, strawberries, mint, and lemon syrup and muddle to combine the ingredients. Add the cachaça and bitters, fill the shaker with ice, and shake until chilled. Double-strain into an ice-filled highball glass. Top off with the Limonata and garnish with a spear of the blueberries and strawberry halves and a mint sprig.

Makes 1 drink

6 blueberries

2 strawberries, stemmed and halved

3 sprigs fresh mint

1/2 ounce Lemon Syrup (see recipe)

2 ounces cachaça

2 dashes Bittermens Boston Bittahs or homemade Grapefruit Bitters (page 62)

San Pellegrino Limonata

Garnish: 2 blueberries, 1 strawberry, stemmed and halved, and 1 sprig fresh mint

LEMON SYRUP

In a medium saucepan, bring the sugar, water, and lemon zest to a simmer, stirring occasionally to dissolve the sugar. At the first crack of a boil, remove from the heat. Once cooled, pour the syrup through a strainer, discard the lemon zest, and store in a glass jar. The syrup will keep in the refrigerator for up to a month.

Makes 1 1/2 cups

1 cup sugar

1 cup water

Zest of 4 lemons

Red Carpet Reviver

Makes 1 drink

---

¹/₂ ounce Blood Orange Syrup
  (see recipe)

1 ounce Aperol

1 ounce Lillet Blanc

1 dash orange bitters

1 dash grapefruit bitters

Chilled Champagne

Garnish: blood orange twist

My friend Terry, a confirmed bachelor of a certain age, is fond of announcing, for no particular reason, "I *am* big! It's the *pictures* that got small." When you catch a Saturday matinee with Terry, as soon as the credits begin to roll, he's ready to hit another theater on the other side of town. The Academy Awards are like Christmas and his birthday rolled into one, but he isn't one to tolerate the typical Oscar party, where the guests are more interested in "Who are you wearing?" than in who's going to win Best Supporting Actress. So instead, Terry hosts an Oscar brunch, which allows him to honor the day among friends, while guaranteeing his guests are out the door by the time the preshow countdown starts. And, if there are any stragglers, Terry sends them on their way by tapping on his watch and announcing "tick-tock, tick-tock."

When I finally made the A-list for his Oscar brunch, he told me he would have Champagne on hand for mimosas, but I threw some additional ingredients in my kit in order to mix up a signature drink in honor of the occasion. The orange-forward flavors of this daytime kicker serve as tribute to those neglected mimosas. The slight bitterness of the Aperol, the orange notes of the bittersweet Lillet, and the blood orange syrup introduce the right amount of red carpet glamour to any Sunday brunch, whether it calls for black tie or frayed pajamas.

Combine the blood orange syrup, Aperol, Lillet, and bitters in a mixing glass filled with ice and stir until chilled. Strain into a chilled double old-fashioned glass filled with ice. Top off with Champagne and garnish with the blood orange twist.

BLOOD ORANGE SYRUP

If blood oranges are out of season you can use freshly squeezed
orange juice, adding some pomegranate juice and a splash of
grenadine to taste.

In a medium saucepan, bring the sugar, water, and blood
orange zest and juice to a boil, stirring occasionally to dissolve
the sugar. At the first crack of a boil, remove from the heat.
Once cooled, pour the syrup through a strainer, discard the
orange zest, and store in a glass jar. The syrup will keep in the
refrigerator for a few days.

Makes 1¹/₂ cups

1 cup sugar

1 cup water

*Zest and juice of 2 blood
oranges*

Sawyer

Makes 1 drink

2 ounces gin, preferably
  Beefeater

$^{1}/_{2}$ ounce freshly squeezed
  lime juice

$^{1}/_{2}$ ounce simple syrup
  (page 92)

14 dashes Angostura bitters

7 dashes Peychaud's Bitters

7 dashes orange bitters,
  preferably equal parts
  Fee Brothers West Indian
  Orange Bitters and Regans'
  Orange Bitters No. 6

I first encountered the Sawyer after a late-night gustatory marathon at Momofuku Ko, the twelve-stool East Village restaurant famous for its elaborate and inventive *omakase*-style tasting menu and a sometimes confounding online reservation system. Even though I had been served far too many courses to remember—the scribbles in my Moleskine notebook that night went from their normal, barely legible state to cave paintings—I left not with a sense of overstuffed food coma, but rather an enlightened eater's high. Despite the subzero temperatures that bitter January night, I wasn't ready to call it quits just yet. A nightcap seemed in order, so I walked over to Ko's sister restaurant, Ssäm Bar.

Don Lee, who spent time at PDT and was then the bar manager for the Momofuku empire, was behind the stick at Ssäm Bar that night, and when I told him I was looking for a post-Ko digestif, he went to work and presented me with the Sawyer, an icy, bitters-soaked twist on a gimlet doctored with nearly thirty dashes of bitters. Don explained that the drink was inspired by wd-50 chef Wylie Dufresne (who loves gin) and was named after Wylie's daughter. The Sawyer is no longer on the menu at Ssäm Bar, but ask nicely and most of the bartenders will know what you're after.

Combine all the ingredients in a cocktail shaker filled with ice and shake until chilled. Double-strain into a chilled double old-fashioned glass.

Scuppernong Sour

Makes 1 drink

---

2 ounces bourbon

*2 tablespoons scuppernong
or muscadine jelly, jam, or
preserves*

*³/₄ ounce freshly squeezed
lemon juice*

*¹/₄ ounce simple syrup
(page 92)*

*2 dashes Fee Brothers
Whiskey Barrel–Aged
Bitters or Angostura bitters*

1 egg white

One of my favorite traditions of the Southern Foodways Alliance Symposium, the annual gathering of writers, chefs, restaurateurs, academics, and serious eaters held annually each fall in Oxford, Mississippi, is the Friday front-porch fried catfish feed that takes place at Taylor Grocery. Part of the experience is the bus ride out to Taylor, where the mode of transportation used to be two open-air double-decker buses that shot through the moonlit countryside like a Deep South version of Mr. Toad's Wild Ride, with hip flasks of brown whiskey passed back and forth as tree branches whizzed by overhead. The double-deckers have been retired, with orange school buses taking their place, but the spirit is still there (as are the spirits).

The sign at Taylor Grocery reads "Eat or We Both Starve," and no one leaves hungry, that's for certain. During my first trip there I spied a stack of homemade preserves by the cash register and left with two pints of scuppernong jelly, something I couldn't easily find back home. While often used interchangeably with muscadine, scuppernong is a variety of the thick-skinned, slightly musky muscadine grape. Native to the southeastern states, scuppernongs come in hues from light green to bronze, while muscadines are typically a reddish-purple.

Both varieties can be enjoyed straight off the vine, reduced to a syrupy glaze, baked into a pie, or made into country wine. North Carolina's ever-inventive Full Steam Brewery even makes a scuppernong sparkling ale. Taking a cue from the marmalade sour, a drink made popular by barman Jamie Boudreau, I've sweetened things up with two spoonfuls of scuppernong jelly and a healthy pour of bourbon. Shaken to within an inch of its life, the result is a frothy tipple that will bring a pucker to your lips.

Combine all the ingredients in a cocktail shaker and dry shake (without ice) to fully incorporate the egg white. Add ice and shake again until chilled. Double-strain into a chilled old-fashioned or coupe glass.

Shady Lane

"Blind date with a chancer, we had oysters and dry Lancers" begins the Pavement classic "Shady Lane." As far as this warm-weather cooler is concerned, the song's refrain says it all: "A Shady Lane, everybody wants one."

Muddling the aromatic shiso leaves (found at Japanese markets), which taste something like a cross between mint and basil, lends a peppery element to this sweet-tart cocktail. The drink is also a tip of the hat to one of my favorite haunts, Momofuku Ssäm Bar, where David Chang keeps Pavement in heavy rotation, and where shiso pops up in both the food and the drink menus. In fact, Pavement bassist Mark Ibold is a bit of a gastronaut himself. In addition to playing with Sonic Youth and dabbling in freelance food styling, he also holds down a gig as bartender at the Great Jones Cafe in the East Village. Maybe if you see him and you ask very nicely, he'll make you your own Shady Lane.

Muddle the syrup, shiso leaves, and blackberries in the bottom of a shaker. Fill with ice, then add the gin, Lillet, lime juice, and bitters. Shake until well chilled, then strain into a chilled double old-fashioned glass filled with cracked ice and top with seltzer. Garnish with the shiso leaf and blackberries.

Makes 1 drink

½ ounce Blackberry-Lime Syrup (see recipe)

3 shiso leaves

3 blackberries

1½ ounces gin

¾ ounce Lillet Rouge

½ ounce freshly squeezed lime juice

2 dashes Scrappy's Lime Bitters or homemade Key Lime Bitters (page 66)

Seltzer

Garnish: 1 shiso leaf and 3 blackberries

BLACKBERRY-LIME SYRUP

In a medium saucepan, combine the sugar, water, blackberries, and lime zest and bring to a simmer, stirring occasionally to dissolve the sugar and pressing the blackberries against the side of the pan with the back of a wooden spoon. At the first crack of a boil, remove from the heat. Once cooled, pour the syrup through a strainer, discard the solids, and store in a glass jar. The syrup will keep in the refrigerator for up to a month.

Makes 1½ cups

1 cup sugar

1 cup water

1 cup blackberries

Zest of 2 limes

Sorghum Flip

Makes 1 drink

———

2 ounces bourbon

½ ounce buttermilk

1 egg

3 tablespoons chopped toasted pecans

Pinch of cinnamon

1 teaspoon brown sugar

1 tablespoon sorghum syrup or molasses

2 dashes homemade Coffee-Pecan Bitters (page 60) or Fee Brothers Whiskey Barrel–Aged Bitters

Garnish: freshly grated nutmeg

Meant to evoke a cold slice of pecan pie eaten straight out of the refrigerator, this Southern-inspired flip incorporates the sweet nuttiness of toasted pecans, bourbon, and the not-so-secret ingredient, sorghum syrup. Similar to molasses, sorghum syrup is a thick, caramel-colored natural sweetener that has a fruity, grassy flavor. Often used interchangeably with molasses, it's great as a topping for warm biscuits, stirred into hot cereal, or as a sweetener in baked goods. I keep my pantry stocked with a cache of sorghum I stumbled upon at a general store attached to a pumpkin farm in Snohomish, Washington, but you can find it at many grocery stores or order it online.

———

Combine all the ingredients except the garnish in a shaker and dry shake (without ice) to incorporate the egg. Fill the shaker with ice and continue to shake until chilled. Double-strain into a chilled old-fashioned glass. Dust with freshly grated nutmeg.

Tipsy Nissley

My friend and former colleague Tom Nissley is many things:
a devoted husband and father to two adorable shaggy-haired
boys, an obsessive reader, an unabashed Jimmy Connors fan,
a record-setting *Jeopardy!* champion, and a lover of that classic
iced-tea-and-lemonade combo, the Arnold Palmer. When I was
thinking of a drink for Nissley, I knew that simply spiking
an Arnold Palmer wouldn't do. Tea-infused bourbon is the
foundation for the drink, but what really makes it is the
smoked citrus I adapted from a technique I picked up from Kat
Kinsman, the managing editor at CNN's food blog, *Eatocracy*.

Kat uses a proper outdoor smoker to enrobe the lemons in
a savory smoke, but if (like me) you're making this in an
apartment without a yard, you can use a stovetop smoker
(available online or at a kitchen supply store). Just remember
to crack open the kitchen window and remove the batteries
from any nearby smoke detectors (but don't forget to put them
back in when you're finished!). For this recipe I typically use
whiskey-barrel wood chips. Using other types—pecan, cedar,
cherry, maple, hickory, or apple wood—will bring about subtle
differences in flavor.

A final note: using chocolate bitters here is another nod to
Nissley, who, without fail, would roll into lunch meetings
at work with a bowl of chili and a tiny carton of chocolate
milk . . . a quirky and seemingly unappetizing pairing that
only Nissley could pull off.

Makes 1 drink

---

2 ounces Tea-Infused Bourbon
(page 188)

3 ounces Smoked Lemonade
(page 188)

Seltzer (optional)

2 dashes chocolate or mole
bitters

Garnish: lemon wedge

Combine the tea-infused bourbon and smoked lemonade in
an ice-filled cocktail shaker. Shake until the ingredients are
chilled. Strain into a highball glass filled with crushed ice and
top with seltzer if desired. Add the bitters, and garnish with
the lemon wedge.

TEA-INFUSED BOURBON

Makes 2 cups

—————

2 cups bourbon

2 bags Earl Grey or other black tea

Pour the bourbon into a jar and add the tea bags. Allow to steep for 15 minutes, then remove the tea bags. The tea-infused bourbon will last indefinitely, but for optimum flavor use within a year.

SMOKED LEMONADE

Makes about 1 quart

—————

Enough wood chips to completely cover the bottom of your smoker

6 to 8 large lemons

¹/₂ cup simple syrup (page 92), or more as needed

6 cups seltzer, or more as needed

Soak the wood chips in tap water to cover for 30 minutes. Remove the chips from the water and line the bottom of your smoker with them. Slice the lemons in half and lay them across the smoking grate, flesh side down. Place the smoker on a single burner over medium heat. Once the wood chips begin to emit wisps of smoke, seal the smoker and smoke the lemons for at least 30 minutes and up to an hour—they should be soft and still have some give. Remove from the heat and allow to cool before opening the smoker. Juice the lemons into a glass jar with a lid. Measure out ¹/₂ cup smoked lemon juice. Save the rest for another use.

Combine the ¹/₂ cup smoked lemon juice and the simple syrup in a 2-quart glass pitcher and stir. Taste and adjust the ratio of lemon juice to simple syrup to reach your preferred balance of sweet and sour, then add enough seltzer to reach your preferred level of smokiness.

Tombstone

Makes 1 drink

2 ounces 100- or 101-proof
  rye

¹⁄₄ ounce rich syrup
  (page 92)

2 dashes Angostura bitters

Garnish: lemon twist

On October 3, 2004, while conducting research for *Imbibe!*, his now-famous biography of cocktail progenitor Jerry Thomas, author David Wondrich led a troop of bartenders and writers on a field trip to the Woodland Cemetery in the Bronx to seek out Thomas's grave. Along with a bag of ice, Wondrich packed a bottle of rye, bitters, sugar, thirteen cocktail glasses, and a cocktail shaker. As Wondrich would be quick to point out, normally you would stir an all-spirits drink like this, but just as the cocktail shaker was passed around that October day, with each person in the party giving it a ceremonial shake, you, too, should shake your Tombstone in honor of Jerry Thomas.

Combine the rye, rich syrup, and bitters in an ice-filled cocktail shaker. Shake until the ingredients are well chilled. Strain into a chilled cocktail glass and garnish with the lemon twist.

Trident

Makes 1 drink

1 ounce dry sherry

1 ounce Cynar

1 ounce aquavit

2 dashes Fee Brothers peach
  bitters

The Trident, considered one of cocktail expert Robert Hess's most successful original cocktails, starts as a Negroni variation, but ends by bringing three seemingly disparate ingredients together with the help of a couple dashes of peach bitters. In fact, this cocktail came about when Hess was working with Fee Brothers, attempting to come up with new cocktail recipes that would take advantage of their unique peach bitters. You can find the Trident on the menu at the Zig Zag Café, one of Hess's favorite Seattle bars, where they burn through more bottles of Cynar, the bittersweet artichoke-based Italian aperitif, than any other bar in Washington state.

Combine all the ingredients in a mixing glass filled with ice. Stir until chilled. Strain into a chilled cocktail glass.

Turkey Shoot

This boozy blunderbuss of a cocktail is the perfect autumnal tipple. Think crackling leaves underfoot on a city sidewalk, weekend football games, and crisp apples eaten out of hand. The spicy rye and the classic fall flavors of the allspice dram (also known as pimento dram) make a welcome base for a slug of apple cider and cinnamon syrup. The slightly bitter Italian vermouth Punt e Mes brings some additional nuance to the drink, and the whiskey and cranberry bitters give it an aromatic kick.

⁓

Combine all the ingredients except the garnish in an ice-filled cocktail shaker and shake until chilled. Strain into a chilled double old-fashioned glass filled with one large cube of ice. Garnish with the lemon zest.

Makes 1 drink

⁓

1¹/₂ ounces 101-proof Wild Turkey rye

¹/₂ ounce Punt e Mes

¹/₄ ounce St. Elizabeth Allspice Dram

³/₄ ounce Cider Reduction (page 192)

¹/₂ ounce Cinnamon Syrup (page 192)

¹/₄ ounce freshly squeezed lemon juice

1 dash Fee Brothers Whiskey Barrel–Aged Bitters

1 dash cranberry bitters

Garnish: thick piece of lemon zest

CIDER REDUCTION

Makes ¹/₂ cup

---

1 cup apple cider

In a small saucepan, bring the apple cider to a boil and cook until the liquid is reduced by half, about 30 minutes. Allow to cool before using. The reduction will keep in the refrigerator for up to a week.

CINNAMON SYRUP

Makes 1¹/₂ cups

---

1 cup water

1 cup sugar

4 cinnamon sticks

In a medium saucepan, combine the water, sugar, and cinnamon stick. Bring to a simmer, stirring occasionally to dissolve the sugar. At the first crack of a boil, remove from the heat. Once cooled, remove the cinnamon sticks and store the syrup in a glass jar. The syrup will keep in the refrigerator for up to a month.

White Light/White Heat

First things first: even if it's served in a Mason jar, that corn whiskey you're nipping isn't technically moonshine unless it was birthed from an illegal still. But, moonshine or not, don't be surprised if the outlaw spirit washes over you when you're drinking the "white dog" (a nickname for white whiskey, an unaged distilled whiskey that remains untouched by the barrel that typically gives whiskey its color). Max Watman wrote a very entertaining book on the topic—*Chasing the White Dog: An Amateur Outlaw's Adventures in Moonshine*—and I hope this is a drink Max would approve of.

Many white whiskey drinks have names like the Corn Popper or the Hillbilly Highball, but I tried to give my concoction a more urbane, sophisticated twist and a name to match. The "white light" comes from the Dolin Vermouth de Chambéry Blanc, which possesses a bittersweet alpine wash, while the "white heat" sneaks up on you from the corn whiskey.

I prefer Kings County Distillery's corn whiskey here—a newer label based out of a loft in Williamsburg, Brooklyn. They opened in April 2010 and are the first whiskey distillery in New York City since Prohibition. Plus, their whiskey comes in a glass hip flask, which I know Max would appreciate. Do avoid any novelty brands, like Georgia Moon, and stick with a small-batch beauty like Tuthilltown's Hudson New York Corn Whiskey or the Finger Lakes Distilling Company's "Glen Thunder" New York Corn Whiskey, both available online.

Makes 1 drink

———

2 ounces corn whiskey

³/₄ ounce Dolin Vermouth de Chambéry Blanc

1 tablespoon chopped candied ginger

2 dashes orange bitters

Garnish: orange twist

Combine all the ingredients except the garnish in a cocktail shaker filled with ice. Shake until chilled. Double-strain into a chilled cocktail glass. Garnish with the orange twist.

Woodland Sunset

Makes 1 drink

---

1 1/2 ounces añejo tequila

*1/4 ounce Lime Syrup
    (see recipe)*

*1 dash Bitter End Moroccan
    Bitters*

San Pellegrino Aranciata

*1/4 ounce pomegranate
    molasses*

Garnish: lime wedge

On July 24, 2002, director Wes Anderson sat in as guest host on *Charlie Rose*. His guest for the night was the legendary, and legendarily eccentric, film producer Robert Evans, best known for helping bring *Love Story* and *The Godfather* to the silver screen. At one point in the interview Anderson asked Evans, "If somebody tells me they really like my tie, what should I do?" Without missing a beat, Evans responded, "If one person tells you they like your tie, that's okay. If five or six people tell you they like your tie, take it home and shred it. Because background makes foreground. If five people tell me they like my shirt, I'll never wear it again. Because the shirt's there to make me look good. Your tie's there to make you look good."

A classic Evans quote, yes, but it's also a great metaphor for how bitters work their magic in a drink. Unless you're drinking something meant to impart bitterness, like the Sawyer (page 181), bitters are background players that step aside and let the drink itself be the star. The spicy Moroccan bitters used here lends a touch of the exotic, just like the sterling silver bolo tie Evans wears—the one he bought from a belly dancer in London for $1,000. This twist on the tequila sunrise is named after Evans's Beverly Hills estate, but it is also a nod to young Evans's role as bullfighter Pedro Romero in the 1957 film version of *The Sun Also Rises*, the part that caused producer Darryl Zanuck to announce through a bullhorn, "The kid stays in the picture. And anybody who doesn't like it can quit."

Build the tequila, lime syrup, and bitters in a highball glass filled with ice. Top off with the Aranciata and stir. Drizzle the pomegranate molasses into the drink and garnish with the lime wedge.

LIME SYRUP

In a medium saucepan, bring the sugar, water, and lime zest to a simmer, stirring occasionally to dissolve the sugar. At the first crack of a boil, remove from the heat. Once cooled, pour the syrup through a strainer, discard the lime zest, and store in a glass jar. The syrup will keep in the refrigerator for up to a month.

Makes 1¹/₂ cups

1 cup sugar

1 cup water

Zest of 6 limes

Zim Zala Bim

Jamie Boudreau came to create the Zim Zala Bim after being intrigued by the nineteenth-century cocktail the Alabazam, particularly its use of a "boatload of bitters." Boudreau took the teaspoon of Angostura in the Alabazam and doubled down with two teaspoons of orange bitters to create this drink. Boudreau insists on using a complex orange bitters for this drink and recommends Regans' Orange Bitters No. 6, since the spicy cardamom notes from Regans' play well with the reposado tequila. It's a drink with "zippy complexity" that will keep the attention of the jaded tequila drinker who is tired of yet another margarita.

Makes 1 drink

2 ounces Partida reposado tequila

2 teaspoons of Regans' Orange Bitters No. 6

2 teaspoons St. Germain elderflower liqueur

1 teaspoon superfine sugar

Lemon twist

Combine all the ingredients except for the lemon twist in a mixing glass and stir until the sugar is dissolved. Fill the mixing glass with ice and continue to stir until chilled. Strain into a chilled cocktail glass. Squeeze the oil from the lemon twist over the drink. Discard the lemon twist and serve.

BITTERS
IN THE
KITCHEN

"I find I do not have indigestion when I use Angostura for my meat sauces."

Mrs. P. H. Klingensmith
1218 Coal Street
Wilkinsburg, PA

—FROM *ANGOSTURA: DELICIOUS-DIGESTIBLE* (DATE UNKNOWN)

The 1960 recipe booklet *The Secret of Good Taste: The Angostura Cook Book* champions the practice of adding a dash of bitters to your everyday cooking to give it a splash of international flair: "The use of Angostura bitters in food, though, has been growing rapidly since smart homemakers discovered that it was the magic ingredient that could transform inexpensive everyday dishes into wonderfully exotic fare."

As it does for cocktails, Angostura can add a delightful dimension to a dish. And, as when making a drink, adding a splash to your food won't necessarily make it taste bitter, but instead can enhance the flavor and aroma. The makers of Angostura introduced cooking with bitters to homemakers in the mid-1900s through advertorial pamphlets and booklets, promising that a dash or two of Angostura was "the secret to good taste" in everything from appetizers to desserts. These booklets included *Angostura: Famous for Foods* (1934), *Angostura: The Secret of Better Taste* (1961), and *Angostura: From Everyday to Gourmet* (1968). As well, pamphlets such as *Angostura: Lively Recipes That Hold the Secret of Better Taste for People Who Are Losing Weight* and *Angostura: Low Sodium Recipes with High Appetite Appeal* harkened back to bitters' medicinal origins.

Using Angostura in the kitchen makes sense when you consider that, despite containing 44.7 percent alcohol, Angostura is classified as a food product. Depending on what state you live in, you might be more likely to find it at a grocery store than a liquor store, shelved in the mixers aisle next to the Rose's lime juice, jars of maraschino cherries and cocktail onions, and flavored margarita salts. At my local grocery store here in Brooklyn, the Angostura is tucked away on a bottom shelf, sandwiched among bottles of fish sauce, pomegranate molasses, and Pickapeppa sauce.

Many of the finished dishes in vintage Angostura advertisements seem like prime material for *The Gallery of Regrettable Food*. Some recipes, like

Pirate Bean Soup, allude to Angostura's home base in the Caribbean, while others, like Fish in-Foil with Flavor, Baked Meat Ring, Company Creamed Chicken, and Prune Chiffon Melva, are simply, well . . . of the era, to put it politely. And I'm still not sure what's going on with a dessert called Santa's Snowballs. Throughout the pamphlets and booklets, you'll discover that most of the recipes call for ingredients and mixes from cans, boxes, and packets. Soup-on-the-Rocks—condensed beef broth over ice with a dash of Angostura—didn't seem to catch on, despite the promise that it was "fast becoming a favorite summertime beverage." And the suggestion that "hash becomes a party dish when Angostura-flavored" seems ready-made for a bumper sticker.

The recipes that follow have been filtered through the prism of the modern kitchen, but some dishes, like the Broiled Bitter Grapefruit, offer a respectful nod to those vintage Angostura recipes. In most instances, however, you don't even need a recipe to take advantage of the concentrated flavor of bitters. Just add a dash to stews, soups, sauces, and gravies. Some of the Fee Brothers bitters, such as rhubarb, cherry, peach, and lemon, seem destined as a pick-me-up for frostings and icings. And chocolate dishes such as fondue or hot fudge would certainly welcome a few dashes of orange bitters. I even like to shake the Angostura bottle over roasted vegetables that I toss with olive oil, salt, and pepper.

More and more craft bartenders are becoming inspired by fresh seasonal ingredients and techniques that traditionally have been relegated to the kitchen. I say that it's time for the bartenders to return the favor, opening chefs' eyes to the culinary possibilities of bitters. Having tasted a foie gras dish capped with an Angostura gelée at the Seattle restaurant Tavern Law, I can say that Angostura's goal of having two bottles in every home—one for the bar and one for the pantry—doesn't seem too far-fetched.

Broiled Bitter Grapefruit

The bitters-splashed grapefruit was a fixture in Angostura recipe guides from 1906 through the 1960s. You'll even find two versions: Anyday Grapefruit and Party-Day Grapefruit. The latter version gets a turn under the broiler and calls for some knife work, as well as artfully arranging alternating orange and grapefruit segments and "radiating them from the center in a flower fashion." This update is more in tune with the broiled grapefruit that's been popping up on restaurant brunch menus lately. Adding bitters to the breakfast table also serves as a wink and a nudge to anyone who might be seeking a little hair of the dog. If you're still suffering the effects from the previous night, then you might not be in the mood to fire up the broiler, but you can accomplish the necessary caramelization with a kitchen torch—just don't catch your robe on fire. If you like, you can garnish each half with a (real) maraschino cherry.

Makes 1 or 2 servings

1 pink or ruby red grapefruit, chilled

Angostura bitters, Peychaud's Bitters, or other aromatic bitters

1 tablespoon melted butter

2 tablespoons Demerara or turbinado sugar

Garnish: maraschino cherry (optional)

Preheat the broiler and cover a baking sheet with aluminum foil.

Slice the grapefruit in half at its equator. Run the knife along the perimeter of each exposed half and along the membrane of each segment to loosen the segments. Dot each grapefruit half with 2 or 3 dashes of bitters.

In a small bowl, mix together the melted butter, sugar, and 6 healthy dashes of bitters to form a sugary paste. Cover each grapefruit half equally with the brown sugar–bitters mixture and place on the prepared baking sheet. Broil until the sugar starts to crisp up and bubble, 2 to 4 minutes. Serve at once.

Sweet & Spicy
Bitter Bar Nuts

Makes 4 cups

———

4 cups mixed unsalted raw nuts, preferably a mix of cashews, pecans, walnuts, and almonds

¼ cup firmly packed light brown sugar

2 tablespoons unsalted butter, melted

2 tablespoons finely chopped fresh rosemary

1 teaspoon cayenne pepper

1 teaspoon ground cinnamon

1 tablespoon honey

1 tablespoon Angostura or other aromatic bitters

1 tablespoon Maldon sea salt (or coarse sea salt or kosher salt)

For years I've served a cayenne- and honey-laced almond mix when I have people over for drinks or dinner, but this next recipe is a riff on (and, really, a tribute to) the two addictive nut mixes served at the bar of Danny Meyer's Gramercy Tavern and Union Square Café (and featured in Meyer's cocktail collection *Mix Shake Stir*). The bitters play backup in this sweet, salty, spicy, impossible-to-push-away party snack. Even if you don't reach for another cocktail, there's no doubt you'll be reaching for another handful of nuts.

———

Preheat the oven to 350°F.

Spread the nuts on a baking sheet and toast in the oven for 10 minutes, giving the pan a shake at the 5-minute mark.

While the nuts are toasting, combine the brown sugar, butter, rosemary, cayenne, cinnamon, honey, and bitters in a large bowl. Add the warm nuts to the bowl and mix them to thoroughly coat. Add the salt and mix again.

The nuts are best served warm, but they can be stored in an airtight container for a few days should you have any left over.

Compound Bitters Butters

Compound butters are simple to make and lend themselves to many sweet and savory applications. Top off a sizzling rib-eye with a knob of aromatic bitters butter, glide a coin of Peychaud's butter across a grilled salmon fillet, or stir a pat of orange bitters butter made with the optional pecans into a bowl of hot oatmeal. The richness of the butter prevents the bitters from cutting to the front of the line while simultaneously bringing a hard-to-place accent to the whole affair. Use the same basic technique for each list of ingredients below.

SAVORY AROMATIC BITTERS BUTTER

$1/2$ cup unsalted butter

1 tablespoon chopped fresh flat-leaf parsley

1 tablespoon Angostura or other aromatic bitters

$1/4$ teaspoon Maldon sea salt (or coarse sea salt or kosher salt)

3 or 4 grinds of black pepper

SWEET AROMATIC BITTERS BUTTER

$1/2$ cup unsalted butter

1 tablespoon Angostura or other aromatic bitters

$1/2$ teaspoon ground cinnamon

$1/4$ teaspoon freshly grated nutmeg

ORANGE BITTERS BUTTER

¹/₂ cup unsalted butter

1 tablespoon orange bitters

¹/₄ teaspoon grated orange zest

Pinch of kosher salt

¹/₄ cup finely chopped toasted pecans (optional)

PEYCHAUD'S BITTERS BUTTER

¹/₂ cup unsalted butter

1 tablespoon Peychaud's bitters

¹/₄ teaspoon grated lemon zest

Pinch of kosher salt

Allow the butter to come to room temperature so it's malleable but not beginning to melt. Combine the butter and all the remaining ingredients in a bowl and mash together with a fork until the ingredients are fully incorporated.

Scoop the butter mixture from the bowl and place in the center of a piece of wax paper. Using your hands, mold the butter into a log shape, and fold the wax paper around the butter to further shape into a cylinder. Twist the ends of the wax paper, like a taffy wrapper, to seal in the butter. Chill in the refrigerator, then store in the freezer, slicing off a thick coin of seasoned butter as needed.

Bitters Vinaigrette

Makes about 1 cup

¾ cup extra-virgin olive oil

¼ cup white wine, cider, or balsamic vinegar

1 tablespoon freshly squeezed lemon juice

1 tablespoon Dijon mustard

1 teaspoon Angostura or other aromatic bitters

Kosher salt to taste

Freshly ground black pepper to taste

By keeping a few basic pantry staples on hand you'll be able to say goodbye to bottled salad dressings and whip up a basic vinaigrette at a moment's notice. Adding bitters to the mix punches up the flavors while introducing a slight blush to the vinaigrette. The basic ratio to work with is 3:1 oil to acid, although there's plenty of wiggle room for experimenting, and you might like to ramp up the lemon juice and dial down the vinegar. You can even sweeten things up with a spoonful of honey.

Combine all the ingredients in a pint Mason jar and shake them until emulsified. Alternatively, you can combine all the ingredients except in the olive oil in a bowl and whisk to combine. Add the olive oil in a steady stream, whisking constantly, until emulsified. The vinaigrette can be stored in a jar in the refrigerator for up to a month.

Bourbon-Bitters Holiday Ham Glaze

In that glorious stretch of overindulgent eating between Christmas and New Year's Day, I always look forward to a sweet and smoky glazed city ham as the centerpiece of the holiday table. This super-easy glaze will have you tossing those prefab packets that come with your ham right in the trash. Start painting the ham with this glaze in the last half hour of cooking time, making sure to reserve some of the warm glaze to pass at the table to drizzle over the slices.

Combine all the ingredients in a medium saucepan and bring to a simmer over medium-low heat. Keep warm until ready to use.

Makes about 2 cups

2 cups firmly packed brown sugar

$^1/_2$ cup blackstrap molasses

$^1/_4$ cup bourbon

$^1/_2$ cup apple cider

2 tablespoons Dijon mustard

2 tablespoons cider vinegar

2 tablespoons Angostura bitters

Zest and juice of 1 orange

Chinese-Style Takeout Ribs with Lacquered Bitters Glaze

Makes 2 to 4 servings

---

¹/₂ cup hoisin sauce

¹/₃ cup soy sauce

3 tablespoons honey

1 tablespoon Sriracha sauce

¹/₄ teaspoon Chinese five-spice powder

2 cloves garlic, minced

1 tablespoon peeled and grated fresh ginger

1 tablespoon cider vinegar

2 tablespoons Angostura or other aromatic bitters

1 rack of pork spareribs (2 to 4 pounds)

While out at a Chinese restaurant in Seattle, my friend Paul ordered the chop suey, announcing, "What the hell. I haven't had it in years, but it sounds like something Jack Lemmon would order." I have to say I feel the same way about Chinese restaurant spareribs: there's a certain nostalgic quality to them. When I was growing up, ordering Chinese takeout was considered a special event. My father never veered from his standard order of shrimp fried rice, but there was always an order of spareribs to pass around the table—and they were always the first dish to disappear.

This is an adaptation of a recipe from *Gourmet* magazine that food writer Nancy Leson featured in her "All You Can Eat" column for the *Seattle Times*. The end result is an aromatic rack with just a touch of heat from the Sriracha and a bit of crunch from the charred glaze. If you have any left over, these also make an amazing late-night snack straight from the icebox.

Combine all of the ingredients except for the spareribs in a bowl and whisk to combine. Set aside ¹/₂ cup of the sauce. Place the ribs in a nonreactive baking dish, pour the sauce on top, and turn to coat the ribs. Marinate in the refrigerator for 1 to 3 hours, turning the ribs once.

Preheat the oven to 400°F and line a rimmed baking sheet with aluminum foil. Place the ribs on the prepared baking sheet and bake for 50 minutes, turning once halfway through the cooking time and basting with half of the reserved sauce. At the end of 50 minutes, remove the ribs from the oven and brush with the remaining sauce.

Preheat the broiler. When hot, broil the ribs, meaty side up, until the ribs begin to char, about 5 minutes. Remove from the broiler, hack the ribs apart with a cleaver or chef's knife, and serve.

Hot & Sticky Bitter Wings

Makes 4 servings

---

¹/₂ cup soy sauce

¹/₄ cup honey

¹/₄ cup Dijon mustard

¹/₂ cup Frank's RedHot Sauce

1 tablespoon Tabasco

*1 tablespoon Angostura or
other aromatic bitters*

¹/₄ cup unsalted butter, melted

2 cloves garlic, chopped

*Freshly ground black pepper
to taste*

*12 whole chicken wings, left
whole or cut in half*

I hail from central New York, just a few Thruway stops away from the birthplace of the mighty Buffalo hot wing. Every pizza parlor and sub shop back home offers hot wings (you wouldn't think of picking up a pizza without an order of hot wings riding shotgun), and none are better than Harpoon Eddie's. This recipe is a sauce-stained salute to the wings of my youth, coated with Frank's RedHot and melted butter. But it has a few twists that I picked up from eating many orders of hot pepper wings—soaked in soy sauce, mustard, garlic, and Tabasco—at the Palace Kitchen in Seattle.

In a large bowl, combine all of the ingredients except the chicken wings. Set aside ¹/₂ cup of the sauce. Place the chicken wings in a large zip-top plastic bag and cover with the sauce. Seal the bag and shimmy the wings around in the sauce to evenly coat. Let the wings hang out in the sauce for 4 to 6 hours; overnight is even better.

Preheat the oven to 425°F and cover a baking sheet with aluminum foil. Place the wings on the baking sheet and bake for 25 minutes. Remove from the oven and brush the wings with the remaining sauce.

Preheat the broiler. When hot, broil the wings until slightly charred, 3 to 4 minutes. Remove from the broiler and serve.

Bitters-and-Balsamic Macerated Strawberries

When strawberry season arrives you can't beat eating them out of hand, but it's also great to have a bowl macerating during dinner on a hot summer night to serve as dessert with a thick spoonful of sweetened whipped cream. Tossing the strawberries with sugar draws out their natural juices, and the balsamic vinegar and bitters add a syrupy, bittersweet zing. In addition to the Angostura, a dash or two of Fee Brothers rhubarb bitters would be a welcome addition here. Serving options abound, but spooned over shortcake, a warm biscuit, or grilled pound cake would be a great place to start.

Wash the strawberries and dry them. Remove the hulls and slice the strawberries in half or in quarters, depending on their size. In a nonreactive bowl, combine the strawberries, brown sugar, vinegar, and bitters and toss gently with a spoon to coat the berries. Cover with plastic wrap and refrigerate for at least 1 hour, until the berries have released their juices to form a syrup. Serve with brown sugar–bourbon whipped cream.

Makes 4 servings

2 pints strawberries

1 tablespoon brown sugar

1 teaspoon balsamic vinegar

6 dashes Angostura bitters

Brown Sugar–Bourbon
 Whipped Cream
 (see recipe)

BROWN SUGAR–BOURBON WHIPPED CREAM

Put the bowl and whisk from your stand mixer (or a bowl and a whisk) in the freezer to chill at least 15 minutes. Remove the chilled equipment from the freezer, add the cream to the bowl, and whisk until the cream begins to thicken. Then add the brown sugar, the bourbon, and the vanilla extract, and whisk until the cream forms stiff peaks.

Makes 1 cup

³/₄ cup cold heavy cream

2 tablespoons light brown sugar

Splash of bourbon

¹/₄ teaspoon vanilla extract

Bitter Apple Fried Hand Pies

Makes 12 hand pies

FOR THE CRUST

2 1/2 cups unbleached all-purpose flour

2 tablespoons sugar

1 teaspoon kosher salt

1/2 cup cold unsalted butter, diced

1/2 cup chilled lard, preferably rendered leaf lard, diced

1/4 cup buttermilk

Growing up, the closest I came to fried pies were the cloying Hostess fruit pies that were a fixture in my grade-school lunchbox. These were a far cry from the fresh-from-the-fryer hand pies I later discovered while traveling through the South—the kind of pies whose unexpected discovery at a roadside gas station could completely change your mood for the better.

The buttermilk crust is from a 1991 *Bon Appétit* recipe, but I've substituted lard for the vegetable shortening. Try to find a tub of rendered leaf lard, the highly prized fat that that surrounds a hog's kidneys. Check with your butcher about ordering a container; it's also available at some farmers' markets. Don't worry: your crust won't have a porky aftertaste, but it will be unforgettably rich and flaky.

Any aromatic bitters or even apple bitters can be used here, but using Fee Brothers Whiskey Barrel–Aged Bitters will give you the classic aromatic profile of clove and nutmeg with a cinnamon kick.

If cooking with hot oil gives you pause, you can also bake these hand pies. Simply place them on a baking sheet lined with parchment paper, cut a small slit in each pie for the steam to escape, and bake at 375°F until golden, about 20 minutes.

To make the crust, in the bowl of a food processor, combine the flour, sugar, and salt and pulse to combine. Add the butter and lard and, with quick bursts of the pulse button, process until the mixture resembles a coarse meal dotted with pea-sized bits of butter and lard. Sprinkle in the buttermilk, 1 tablespoon at a time, and continue to pulse until the dough comes together into a ball. Remove the dough from the food processor and, with floured hands, gently knead several times. Divide the dough into 12 balls of equal size and refrigerate for 30 minutes.

To make the filling, dice the apples into ¹/₂-inch cubes and add to a medium saucepan along with the sugar, butter, cinnamon, nutmeg, salt, lemon juice, bitters, and flour. Cook over medium heat, stirring occasionally, until the apples start to soften and break down a bit, 15 to 20 minutes. Remove from the heat and let cool completely.

Dust a countertop lightly with flour. Press a ball of dough into a disk with the palm of your hand, then, using a floured rolling pin, roll out into a thin disk, 5 to 6 inches in diameter and ¹/₈ inch thick. If you like, you can use a large biscuit cutter or appropriately sized lid to cut out a perfect circle. Place 1 heaping tablespoon of the apple filling in the center of the dough. Using a pastry brush or your fingers, dab the edges of the dough with water. Carefully fold the dough over the filling, press to seal, and crimp the edges with the tines of a fork. Repeat with the remaining balls of dough and filling. Keep the pies chilled in the refrigerator until ready to fry.

To fry the pies, pour the oil into an 8- or 9-inch cast-iron skillet until it reaches a depth of about ¹/₂ inch. Heat the oil over medium-high heat until the temperature reads 375°F on a deep-frying thermometer. Meanwhile, line a baking sheet with paper towels. In batches of three, place the pies in the oil and fry, turning once with a slotted spoon, until the crusts are golden brown, about 3 minutes. Transfer to the paper towels to drain.

To make the glaze, whisk together the confectioners' sugar, buttermilk, vanilla extract, and bitters. Using a pastry brush, brush the warm pies with the glaze. Serve warm.

FOR THE FILLING

3 or 4 large apples, peeled and cored

¹/₄ cup sugar

2 tablespoons unsalted butter

1 teaspoon ground cinnamon

¹/₄ teaspoon freshly grated nutmeg

Pinch of kosher salt

¹/₂ teaspoon freshly squeezed lemon juice

1 teaspoon Fee Brothers Whiskey Barrel–Aged Bitters or other aromatic bitters

1 tablespoon all-purpose flour

Vegetable oil for frying

FOR THE GLAZE

¹/₂ cup confectioners' sugar

1 tablespoon buttermilk

¹/₄ teaspoon vanilla extract

4 dashes Fee Brothers Whiskey Barrel–Aged Bitters or other aromatic bitters

Bitters-Sweet Chocolate Malted Pudding

Makes 6 servings

———

¹/₂ cup sugar

¹/₄ cup unsweetened cocoa powder

3 tablespoons cornstarch

2 cups whole milk

3 egg yolks

6 ounces semisweet chocolate, finely chopped

2 tablespoons unsalted butter

1 teaspoon vanilla extract

1 teaspoon chocolate or mole bitters

¹/₃ cup malted milk powder

Pinch of kosher salt

Sweetened whipped cream (see recipe)

¹/₂ cup crushed malted milk balls

Homey, understated, and often unexpected, pudding is one of my go-to desserts. As an adult, my favorite rendition is served at the Palace Kitchen in Seattle (even if chef Tom Douglas is more famous for his coconut cream pie), but my fondness for chocolate pudding goes back much farther than that, to childhood Sunday suppers. My mother always made dessert first, and while she was preparing the rest of dinner, I'd stare at those six glass goblets of pudding cooling on the countertop, each one bedecked with a walnut. There were five of us in my family, so the question of who would get the bonus pudding was the immediate topic of conversation among my siblings and me. And luckily, as the youngest (or, as my brother and sister might claim, the most spoiled), I often wound up with that leftover pudding.

Malt is one of my favorite flavoring agents. As with bitters, when it's added to a dessert, you can't quickly identify what it is that's making it taste so special. The combination of bitters and puddings dates back to the old Angostura recipe pamphlets, and with good reason: bitters work very well with dense, rich desserts like this, helping the flavors pop while adding an underlying spice note to the thick chocolate custard.

———

In a medium pan, whisk together the sugar, cocoa powder, and cornstarch. Over medium heat, pour in the milk and continue to whisk until the mixture begins to thicken and comes to a boil. Keep at a boil for about 30 seconds. Remove from the heat.

In a large bowl, whisk the egg yolks together. Slowly add 2 tablespoons of the hot milk mixture to the egg yolks, whisking constantly. Gradually whisk in the remaining milk mixture and then whisk in the chocolate, butter, vanilla extract, bitters, malted milk powder, and salt until smooth.

Allow to cool for 10 minutes, whisking occasionally. Pour the pudding into six serving vessels (wide-mouth half-pint Mason jars are a favorite of mine, but you can also use ramekins, old-fashioned glasses, goblets, or coffee mugs). Cover each container with plastic wrap, pressing the plastic wrap against the surface of the pudding to prevent a skin from forming. Refrigerate for at least 4 hours, and ideally overnight.

Serve the pudding with a thick dollop of sweetened whipped cream and a sprinkle of the crushed malted milk balls.

SWEETENED WHIPPED CREAM

Place the bowl and whisk from your stand mixer (or a bowl and a whisk) in the freezer to chill at least 15 minutes. Remove the chilled equipment from the freezer, add the heavy cream to the bowl, and whisk until the cream thickens slightly. Then add the confectioners' sugar and the vanilla extract and whisk until the cream forms stiff peaks.

Makes 1 cup

³/₄ cup cold heavy cream

2 tablespoons confectioners' sugar

¹/₄ teaspoon vanilla extract

Boozy Bitter Granitas

OLD-FASHIONED
GRANITA

Makes 4 to 6 servings

———

2 cups water

*2 cups Demerara or turbinado
sugar*

1 cinnamon stick

*1 tablespoon grated orange
zest*

*1 tablespoon freshly squeezed
orange juice*

3 tablespoons bourbon

2 teaspoons Angostura bitters

1 teaspoon cherry juice

*4 to 6 thick strips of
orange zest*

An icy combination of sugar, fresh juice, and spirits, these granitas are the perfect low-maintenance desserts with a kick. Your freezer does most of the heavy lifting here. As the dessert freezes, you'll run a fork through it every thirty minutes over the course of a few hours, like you're tending a tiny, boozy Zen garden. Served in old-fashioned glasses, these spirited tributes to the classic old-fashioned and New Orleans's storied Sazerac are a great way to wrap up a dinner party with panache.

———

To make the old-fashioned granita: Place a glass or metal 9 by 13-inch pan in the freezer to chill while you prepare the granita.

Combine the water and sugar in a saucepan over medium heat and stir until the sugar is completely dissolved. When it comes to a boil, remove from the heat and stir in the cinnamon stick, orange zest and juice, bourbon, bitters, and cherry juice. Let cool to room temperature.

Strain the mixture into the chilled pan and return to the freezer. After 30 minutes, stir the mixture with a whisk. Return to the freezer for at least 3 hours, removing it every 30 minutes or so and using a fork to scrape the ice crystals to break them up. You can leave the mixture as chunky, crunchy ice crystals, or break up the crystals more for a softer, snowball consistency. Just before serving, give the granita one last fluff with the fork. Serve in short rocks glasses or old-fashioned glasses garnished with the orange zest.

To make the sazerac granita: Place a glass or metal 9 by 13-inch pan in the freezer to chill while you prepare the granita.

Combine the water and sugar in a saucepan over medium heat and stir until the sugar is completely dissolved. When it comes to a boil, remove from the heat and stir in the lemon zest and juice, rye, and bitters. Let cool to room temperature.

SAZERAC GRANITA

Makes 4 to 6 servings

————

2 cups water

2 cups sugar

1 tablespoon grated lemon
zest

2 tablespoons freshly squeezed
lemon juice

3 tablespoons rye

2 teaspoons Peychaud's
bitters

Splash of absinthe, Pernod,
or Herbsaint

4 to 6 thick strips of
lemon zest

Pour the absinthe into the chilled pan and use a pastry brush
to coat the bottom and sides of the pan with the liquid. Strain
the mixture into the chilled pan and return to the freezer.
After 30 minutes, stir the mixture with a whisk. Return to
the freezer for at least 3 hours, removing it every 30 minutes
or so and using a fork to scrape the ice crystals to break
them up. You can leave the mixture as chunky, crunchy ice
crystals, or break up the crystals more for a softer, snowball
consistency. Just before serving, give the granita one last fluff
with the fork. Serve in short rocks glasses or old-fashioned
glasses garnished with the lemon zest.

Aromatic Bitters Ice Cream

Makes 1 quart

---

2 cups heavy cream

1 cup whole milk

³/₄ cup brown sugar

¹/₄ teaspoon kosher salt

4 green cardamom pods

1 vanilla bean

1 cinnamon stick

2 cloves

¹/₂ teaspoon gentian root

¹/₄ teaspoon grated orange
zest

¹/₄ teaspoon freshly grated
nutmeg

6 large egg yolks

¹/₃ cup blackstrap or dark
rum

Angostura bitters

Adding a few splashes of Angostura bitters to a dish of vanilla
ice cream can be a wonderful thing, but doing this got me
thinking about creating an ice cream that didn't necessarily
contain Angostura but instead alluded to Dr. Siegert's top-
secret bitters. The cream and milk soak up just enough of the
aromatics, which include bitter gentian root, and a splash of
blackstrap rum at the finish helps brings a rich, high-proof
kick without overpowering the ice cream.

Combine the cream, milk, brown sugar, and salt in a saucepan
and slowly bring to a simmer over medium-low heat, stirring
occasionally.

Meanwhile, crack the cardamom pods using a mortar and
pestle or the bottom of a heavy mug. Split the vanilla bean
lengthwise with a small, sharp knife.

When the cream mixture starts to simmer, remove from the
heat. Add the cracked cardamom pods, scrape the vanilla
seeds from the bean halves into the liquid, and add the bean
halves. Add the cinnamon stick, cloves, gentian root, orange
zest, and nutmeg and stir to combine. Cover and let steep
for 45 minutes, then strain the cream through a fine-mesh
sieve. Discard the solids and return the cream mixture to the
saucepan over medium-low heat.

In a bowl, whisk together the egg yolks, then slowly pour in the warm cream mixture in batches, whisking constantly. Pour the custard back into the saucepan and return to medium-low heat, whisking constantly. Continue cooking the custard, without allowing it to come to a boil, until the custard is thick enough to coat the back of a spoon (if you run a finger along the back of that custard-coated spoon, the impression should remain there).

Strain the custard through a fine-mesh sieve into a bowl to remove any bits of egg solids or errant aromatics. Stir in the rum, cover with plastic wrap, and chill in the refrigerator for at least 4 hours, or preferably overnight.

Pour the chilled custard into an ice cream maker and churn according to the manufacturer's instructions. It typically takes 15 to 30 minutes, but you want to stop churning when the consistency is still soft, like a Wendy's Frosty. Transfer to a container with a tight-fitting lid and cover the surface of the ice cream with plastic wrap before sealing. Freeze the ice cream until it has hardened, about 2 hours.

Remove from the freezer 15 minutes before serving. Scoop into double old-fashioned glasses and adorn each serving with a dash or two of Angostura bitters.

RESOURCES

BITTERS MAKERS

A.B. Smeby Bittering Co.
www.absmebybitteringco.com

Angostura
www.angostura.com

Bittercube
www.bittercube.com

The Bitter End
www.bitterendbitters.com

Bitter Tears
www.msandhis.com

The Bitter Truth
www.the-bitter-truth.com

Bittermens
www.bittermens.com

Bitters, Old Men
www.bittersoldmen.com

Brooklyn Hemispherical Bitters
www.brooklynbitters.com

Dr. Adam Elmegirab's Boker's Bitters
www.bokersbitters.co.uk

Fee Brothers
www.feebrothers.com

The Sazerac Company
www.sazerac.com

Scrappy's Bitters
www.scrappysbitters.com

Sweetgrass Farm Winery & Distillery
www.sweetgrasswinery.com

Urban Moonshine
www.urbanmoonshine.com

BITTERS, BOOKS, BOTANICALS, AND BARWARE

Amazon.com
www.amazon.com

Bar Keeper Silverlake
www.barkeepersilverlake.com

BevMo!
www.bevmo.com

The Boston Shaker
www.thebostonshaker.com

Cask
www.caskstore.com

Cocktail Kingdom
www.cocktailkingdom.com

Dandelion Botanical Company
www.dandelionbotanical.com

DeLaurenti Specialty Food & Wine
www.delaurenti.com

DrinkUpNY
www.drinkupny.com

Kalustyan's
www.kalustyans.com

KegWorks
www.kegworks.com

The Meadow
www.atthemeadow.com/shop

Pearl Specialty Market & Spirits
www.pearlspecialty.com

Small Hand Foods
www.smallhandfoods.com

Spuyten Duyvil
www.spuytenduyvilnyc.com

Tenzing Momo
www.tenzingmomo.com

Trader Tiki's Hand-Crafted Exotic Syrups
www.tradertiki.com

SPIRITED SITES

A. J. Rathbun
www.ajrathbun.com

Alcademics
www.alcademics.com

Alcohology
www.alcohology.wordpress.com

Ardent Spirits
www.ardentspirits.com

Art of Drink
www.artofdrink.com

Beachbum Berry
www.beachbumberry.com

Beers in the Shower
www.beersintheshower.blogspot
.com

Cask Strength
www.caskstrength.wordpress.com

The Cocktail Chronicles
www.cocktailchronicles.com

Cocktailians
www.cocktailians.com

cocktailnerd
www.cocktailnerd.com

Cocktail Virgin Slut
www.cocktailvirgin.blogspot.com

A Dash of Bitters
www.adashofbitters.com

Drink Boy
www.drinkboy.com

Drink Dogma
www.drinkdogma.com

Ford Mixology Lab
www.fordmixologylab.com

Imbibe Unfiltered
www.imbibemagazine.blogspot.com

Jeffrey Morgenthaler
www.jeffreymorgenthaler.com

King Cocktail
www.kingcocktail.com

Liberty Loves You
www.libertybars.com/blog

Liquidity Preference
www.jacobgrier.com/blog

Meet Dr. Cocktail
www.drcocktail.com

The Modern Mixologist
www.themodernmixologist.com

The Museum of the American Cocktail
www.museumoftheamerican
cocktail.org

NW Vivant
www.nwvivant.com

Oh Gosh!
www.ohgo.sh

Party On Damen
www.partyondamen.wordpress.com

Scofflaw's Den
www.scofflawsden.com

Serious Drinks
www.drinks.seriouseats.com

Sloshed!
www.sloshed.hyperkinetic.org

Slow Cocktails
www.slowcocktails.com

Spirits and Cocktails
www.spiritsandcocktails.wordpress
.com

Stirred Not Shaken
www.stirrednotshakenblog
.wordpress.com

Underhill-Lounge
www.underhill-lounge.flannestad.com

RECOMMENDED READING
FOR THE COCKTAIL ENTHUSIAST

Abou-Ganim, Tony, with Mary Elizabeth Faulkner. *The Modern Mixologist: Contemporary Classic Cocktails*. Berkeley: Agate Surrey, 2010.

Amis, Kingsley. *Everyday Drinking: The Distilled Kingsley Amis*. New York: Bloomsbury USA, 2010.

Arthur, Stanley Clisby. *Famous New Orleans Drinks and How to Mix 'Em*. Gretna, LA: Pelican Publishing, 1977.

Baker, Charles H., Jr. *The Gentleman's Companion Vol. II: Being an Exotic Drinking Book*. New York: Crown, 1946.

Baker, Charles H., Jr. *Jigger, Beaker and Glass*. Lanham and New York: The Derrydale Press, 2001.

Beattie, Scott. *Artisanal Cocktails: Drinks Inspired by the Seasons from the Bar at Cyrus*. Berkeley: Ten Speed Press, 2008.

Boothby, William T. *Cocktail Boothby's American Bartender: The New Anchor Distilling Edition*. San Francisco: Anchor Distilling, 2009.

Craddock, Harry. *The Savoy Cocktail Book*. London: Pavilion Books Limited, 2007.

Crockett, A. S. *The Old Waldorf-Astoria Bar Book* (reprint edition). New Day Publishing, 2003.

Curtis, Wayne. *And a Bottle of Rum: The History of the New World in Ten Cocktails*. New York: Three Rivers Press, 2007.

DeGroff, Dale. *The Craft of the Cocktail*. New York: Clarkson Potter, 2002.

DeGroff, Dale. *The Essential Cocktail*. New York: Clarkson Potter, 2008.

DeVoto, Bernard. *The Hour: A Cocktail Manifesto* (reprint edition). Portland: Tin House Books, 2010.

Embury, David A. *The Fine Art of Mixing Drinks* (revised edition). New York: Mud Puddle Books, 2008.

Field, Colin Peter. *The Cocktails of the Ritz Paris*. New York: Simon & Schuster, 2003.

Grimes, William. *Straight Up or On the Rocks: The Story of the American Cocktail*. New York: North Point Press, 2002.

Haigh, Ted. *Vintage Spirits and Forgotten Cocktails*. Beverley, MA: Quarry Books, 2009.

Hess, Robert. *The Essential Bartender's Guide*. New York: Mud Puddle Books, 2008.

Hollinger, Jeff, and Rob Schwartz. *The Art of the Bar: Cocktails Inspired by the Classics*. San Francisco: Chronicle Books, 2006.

Johnson, Harry. *Harry Johnson's New and Improved Bartenders' Manual and a Guide for Hotels and Restaurants* (reproduction of the 1900 edition). New York: Mud Puddle Books, 2008.

Kosmas, Jason, and Dushan Zaric. *Speakeasy: The Employees Only Guide to Classic Cocktails Reimagined.* Berkeley: Ten Speed Press, 2010.

Mario, Thomas. *Playboy's Host & Bar Book.* Chicago: Playboy Press, 1971.

McGee, Harold. *On Food and Cooking: The Science and Lore of the Kitchen* (revised edition). New York: Scribner, 2004.

Munat, Ted, with Michael Lazar. *Left Coast Libations: The Art of West Coast Bartending.* Oakland: Left Coast Libations, 2010.

Okrent, Daniel. *Last Call: The Rise and Fall of Prohibition.* New York: Scribner, 2010.

Page, Karen, and Andrew Dornenburg. *The Flavor Bible.* New York: Little, Brown & Co., 2008.

Page, Karen, and Andrew Dornenburg. *What to Drink with What You Eat.* New York: Bulfinch Press, 2006.

Rathbun, A. J. *Good Spirits.* Boston: Harvard Common Press, 2007.

Regan, Gary. *The Joy of Mixology.* New York: Clarkson Potter, 2003.

Regan, Gary, and Mardee Haidin Regan. *New Classic Cocktails.* New York: Wiley Publishing, 1997.

Reighley, Kurt B. *United States of Americana: Backyard Chickens, Burlesque Beauties & Handmade Bitters—A Field Guide to the New American Roots Movement.* New York: Harper, 2010.

Thomas, Jerry. *The Bar-Tender's Guide: How to Mix Drinks, or, The Bon Vivant's Companion* (reproduction of the 1862 edition). New York: Mud Puddle Books, 2008.

Watman, Max. *Chasing the White Dog: An Amateur Outlaw's Adventures in Moonshine.* New York: Simon & Schuster, 2010.

Wondrich, David. *Imbibe! From Absinthe Cocktail to Whiskey Smash, A Salute in Stories and Drinks to "Professor" Jerry Thomas, Pioneer of the American Bar.* New York: Perigee, 2007.

Wondrich, David. *Punch: The Delights (and Dangers) of the Flowing Bowl.* New York: Perigee, 2010.

ACKNOWLEDGMENTS

I am forever grateful to Aaron Wehner and Emily Timberlake for their enthusiasm and dedication in taking on this book and helping develop it from proposal to printed page, and I am especially thankful for Emily's expert editorial guidance and saintlike patience. It's an honor to be a part of the Ten Speed family, especially with a talented team like Michele Crim, Patricia Kelly, Colleen Cain, and Kristin Casemore on my side. Sharron Wood, thank you for your copyediting (and cocktail) expertise. And a big thanks to publicist Anna Mintz and everyone at the Crown Publishing Group for their support.

Ed Anderson brought this book to life with his gorgeous photographs and creative design. I encourage anyone who has the chance to run around Manhattan, Brooklyn, and Seattle with Ed and his camera, breaking bread together along the way.

Thanks to my bitters-loving agent, Michael Bourret, who took on this project and first-time author with the utmost confidence.

When I lived in Seattle one of my favorite pastimes was Friday nights at the Palace Kitchen, and it means the world to me that the restaurant played an enormous behind-the-scenes role in the creation of this book. An immeasurable debt of gratitude goes out to the entire Tom Douglas Restaurant Group, especially Tom Douglas and Jackie Cross, Eric Tanaka, Robyn Wolfe, Sean Hartley, Sue Burns, Gretchen Geisness, Brian Walczyk, Garrett and Molly Melkonian, Shelley Lance, Pamela Hinckley, Katie Okumura, Eric Feller, and Sandy Kuala. Thanks for making me feel as if I never moved away.

A very special round of thanks is due to Jim Meehan, who answered every one of my e-mails within minutes and let me slip through the phone booth at PDT before opening hours for unlimited access to his vast knowledge of cocktails and spirits, as well as his stellar bitters collection. An afternoon shooting cocktails at PDT, made by the amazing Jeff Bell and overseen with Jim's obsessive eye for detail, was one of the highlights of completing this project.

David Chang, whose generosity knows no bounds, is a man who means it when he says, "Let me know if there's anything we can do to help." Thanks to Sue Chan for letting us take over Momofuku Ssäm Bar and to John deBary for turning out so many gorgeous cocktails for us to shoot.

A shout-out to Karen Fu, to Christopher Harrington for shaking up a last-minute Sawyer for a pick-up shot, and to Christina Tosi and her Milk Maidens for always keeping me in sweets. Each and every person at Ssäm Bar makes this Friday regular feel very special indeed.

When I moved to New York, my first meal in Brooklyn was at Frankies 457. Since then I've continued to haunt that magical strip of Court Street, bopping between Frankies and Prime Meats on a regular basis. I've been fortunate to get to know Frank Castronovo and Frank Falcinelli, who welcomed me like family. Damon

Boelte at Prime Meats has been an invaluable bitters resource and the man behind some of my favorite drinks in town. If, by the time you're reading this, his pear bitters and Buddha's hand bitters are commercially available, the world will be a better place. Big thanks to the Franks, Christina Knowlton, Travis Kauffman, and Annie Llewellyn for letting us set up shop at Prime Meats for a photo shoot, and to Damon for making so many Champagne Cocktails, Seelbachs, and Sazeracs. And thanks to Max Quattrone, Marci DeLozier Haas, Cabell Tomlinson, Nate Dumas, and all of the bartenders and servers whose constant hospitality knows no bounds.

A special thanks to Kat Spellman, Brian McCracken, Dana Tough, Nathan Weber, and Philip Thompson at Seattle's Tavern Law for their hospitality and access to their magnificent glasses and barware.

New Yorkers were very lucky when Mark and Jennifer Bitterman opened an outpost of their Portland, Oregon, shop, The Meadow, at 523 Hudson Street. And I was thrilled when Mark invited us in during the busy opening weeks to shoot his extensive selection of bitters. New York City's bitters selection has increased tenfold overnight with the arrival of The Meadow.

Thanks to Brian Kern and Mary Kachi Cassinelli at Seattle's Dandelion Botanical Company for welcoming us in to shoot their extensive selection of herbs and botanicals.

And, finally, thanks to Aziz Osmani at Kalustyan's, who let us wander the aisles of his stunning New York City culinary emporium to shoot all of the essential aromatic botanicals, herbs, and spices for making your own bitters at home.

I offer immeasurable depths of gratitude to all of the bartenders and cocktail professionals who answered my many questions and afforded me access to their time, wisdom, and delicious drinks: A. J. Rathbun (who helped set things in motion), David Nelson, David Wondrich, Jamie Boudreau, Robert Hess, Don Lee, Miles Thomas, Andrew Bohrer, Murray Stenson, Joe Fee, Ellen Fee, Adam Elmegirab, Rocky Yeh, Dale DeGroff, Keith Waldbauer, Maggie Savarino, Stephan Berg, Alexander Hauck, Julian Brizzi, Alex Day, Andrew Friedman, Zane Harris, Jay Kuehner, Casey Robison, Jim Romdall, Neyah White, Greg Best, Regan Smith, Michael Rubel, Max Watman, Avery and Janet Glasser, and Anna Wallace.

For their support, encouragement, counsel, and inspiration, I'd like to thank Peter Meehan, Matt Lee and Gia Papini Lee, Ted Lee and E. V. Day, Ethan and Angela Stowell, Mark Fuller and Marjorie Chang Fuller, John T. Edge, Karen Page and Andrew Dornenburg, Thierry Rautureau, Elizabeth Karmel, Danny Meyer, David Pasternack, Armandino and Marilyn Batali, Gina Batali and Brian D'Amato, Roy Finamore, Dorie Greenspan, Ina Garten, Ed Levine, Erin Kathleen Zimmer, Kim Ricketts, Amy Pennington, Kirsten Graham, Patric Gabre-Kidan, Judy Amster, Jessica Voelker, Katherine Koberg, Rebecca Staffel, Kat Kinsman,

Lisa Fain, Rich Tullis, Kelly Leonard, Martha Otis, Laurie Brown, Spenser Lee, Ann Bramson, Will Schwalbe, Dorothy Kalins, Jane Lear, Hugh Andrews, Amy Worley, Christene Barberich, Brian Corona, the Stewart family, Michael Ferch, Ed Nawotka, Ted Blanchard, Marty Gosser, Jen Haller, Patty Berg, Mike Harrington, Eugenia Pakalik, Amy Weinstein and Crasta Yo, Anne Bartholomew, Tom Nissley, Jon Foro, Sean McDonald, Peter Cohen, Jennifer Gilmore, Ryan Boudinot, Kate Kraft, Mindy Ruehmann, Caroline Carr, Dave and Karen Callanan, Daphne Durham and Craig Doberstein, Chris and Stacey Brucia, Mari Malcolm, Terry Goodman, Rob Mulliner, Brooke Gilbert and Bob Gately, Daniel Sheldon, Alex Carr, Gisele Garelik, Paul and Kristin Ford, and Caroline Lee.

Thanks to my family for their love and support: Herbert "Bert" Parsons, whom I miss each and every day, Joanne and Gary Murphy, Vicki, Bob, and Jack Adams, Scott, Becki, and Jacob Parsons, Gary Murphy Jr., and Ryan, Kassie, Kole, and Max Murphy. And Louis.

My sincere apologies to anyone I may have missed, and a promise to pick up the next round.

INDEX

Some of the recipes in this book include raw eggs. When eggs are consumed raw, there is always the risk that bacteria, which is killed by proper cooking, may be present. For this reason, always buy certified salmonella-free eggs from a reliable grocer, storing them in the refrigerator until they are served. Because of the health risks associated with the consumption of bacteria that can be present in raw eggs, they should not be consumed by infants, small children, pregnant women, the elderly, or any persons who may be immunocompromised. The author and publisher expressly disclaim responsibility for any adverse effects that may result from the use or application of the recipes and information contained in this book.

Published in the United States by Ten Speed Press, an imprint of the Crown Publishing Group, a division of Random House, Inc., New York.
www.crownpublishing.com
www.tenspeed.com

Ten Speed Press and the Ten Speed Press colophon are registered trademarks of Random House, Inc.

Library of Congress Cataloging-in-Publication Data
Parsons, Brad Thomas.
  Bitters : a spirited history of a classic cure-all, with cocktails,
recipes, and formulas / Brad Thomas Parsons.
      p. cm.
 1. Cocktails. 2. Bitters. 3. Cookbooks. I. Title.
  TX951.P355 2011
  641.8'74--dc23
                              2011017774

ISBN 978-1-58008-359-1

Printed in China

Design by Ed Anderson

10 9 8 7 6 5 4 3 2

First Edition